Esther

Esther

A NOVEL in VERSE

PAM BERNARD

CavanKerry ◊ Press LTD.

CavanKerry Press Ltd.
Fort Lee, New Jersey
www.cavankerrypress.org

Publisher's Cataloging-in-Publication
(Provided by Quality Books, Inc.)

Bernard, Pam.
Esther : a novel in verse / Pam Bernard. -- First
edition.
pages cm
ISBN 978-1-933880-48-8

1. Mothers and daughters--Fiction. 2. Fathers and
daughters--Fiction. 3. Incest--Fiction. 4. Novels in
verse. 5. Psychological fiction.   I. Title.

PS3552.E7269E88 2015   813'.54
QBI15-600023

Cover photographs courtesy of the Bernard Family Archives and Gregory Smith
Cover and interior text design by Gregory Smith
First Edition 2015, Printed in the United States of America

CavanKerry Press is dedicated to springboarding the careers of previously unpublished, early, and mid-career poets by bringing to print two to three Emerging Voices annually. Manuscripts are selected from open submission; Cavankerry Press does not conduct competitions.

CavanKerry Press is grateful for the support it receives from the New Jersey State Council on the Arts.

This project is supported in part by an award from the National Endowment for the Arts. To find out more about how NEA grants impact individuals and communities, visit www.arts.gov.

To women and girls everywhere—

and to the spirit of survival in us all.

Contents

Prologue 3

Words 5

Garden 25

Big River 37

The Song of the Lark 49

Train 71

Our Bed Is Green 97

Great Divide 109

Weeper 125

Sierras 141

Vuelva a mí 157

Queen of the Meadow 169

Acknowledgments 181

Esther

Prologue

There are only two or three human stories, and they go on repeating themselves as fiercely as if they had never happened before.

—Willa Cather, *O Pioneers!*

*I unfold a map of the country
and smooth it flat on my kitchen table,
hover over it late into the night, struggling*

*to square the circle of my life, the map
a guide to where I have gotten lost.*

*Now I commit to rightly reclaim
its folds, to put this sadness
finally away.*

Words

A is the first letter of the alphabet, because, if pronounced open, as in father *. . . it is the simplest and easiest of sounds. A is the letter with which children generally begin to speak, and it serves to express many and even opposite emotions: pain, pleasure.*

—*Encyclopedia Americana*, 1829

From across the meadow her father
called into the darkening air.   *Esther*

She wanted to yell out, to tell someone,
but a quiet covered her mouth and kept her
still. As the last slender spine of daylight

stabbed through her hiding place, she
began to make her way home. The sky
bled black with crows, hundreds of them,
an argosy of wings banking the horizon.

Mother clamped the meat grinder, her
one-armed household god, to the table's edge—
hash for supper, sweet corn put up
last summer, lustered from the field.

                    All night
wind wrestled the honey locust.
When morning came the horse
ran loose in the peach orchard.

* * *

A small pond appeared that spring
in the middle of the meadow, a single eye
to keep watch.
                    Esther loved more than anything

to lie among the tracery of bittersweet
along its banks and listen for wind.
She'd hold still to hear the faintest rustle,
until, from somewhere in the ribbed

helmet of sky, it came for her, filled her—
and then, as if a hand lifted
from the cage of her chest, it moved
on and let her breathe again.

For as long she could remember Esther
had been able to escape the darkness
her father brought nightly to her room.

So small was she when Aaron first touched her,
she thought it odd that he came so near,
then squirmed as his arm disappeared
to the elbow under her nightdress.

                              Father, your hand . . .

but the giggle caught in her throat
as pain shot up into her belly.

What she could not say she held inside her,
until one night there appeared in her mind
a castle—as she had seen in fairy tales
Miss Hollister read them after lessons—

bright with turrets and banners flying,
the moat around it sparkling, a bridge
to be lowered and raised.

The first time Esther crossed she kept
her head down and followed her feet
to see where they might go.

Sun pressed warm on her shoulders
as she stepped carefully onto the wooden
planks that sang with each footfall.

Water lapped all around, and on the far side,
a bank rose to an opened iron gate.
Tansy swayed in the dooryard.

A great hall led to the keep, the deepest,
safest room, filled with tapestries thick
as rugs, brocade draping a stone bench,
a stone hearth, the fire as tall as she stood.

Then the words came, the few she knew—
from Mother's kitchen garden— lovage,
savory, angelica. Calendula, whose eyes
she imagined were kind, whose
hands were soft and warm.

Words circled the cool marble floors, rising,
unfolding slowly in the air to become
the one sound, a kind of whir of wings, until
it joined her by the fire and held her close.

* * *

The children at school were drawn
to Esther's mournful beauty, her long black
braids, her eyes so dark their pupils were lost.

They chose to linger near her
whenever they could, the teacher
directing her lessons at Esther as if
she were the only student.

Without knowing or questioning why,
they were in her thrall, though Esther knew
none of it, sensed nothing. Perplexed
by her silence, the children would move
away, the girls becoming a snarl

of chatter in one corner or another, but because
Esther would not have felt their presence,
neither would she their leaving.

In her starched white smock, leggings,
and lace-up shoes, she seemed always
at odds with her clothing, her body
struggling in its mute courage against

confinement. From the gathered cuffs
of her blouse sprang her strong hands,
like small startled animals. They calmed
only when she held a book.

* * *

One stormy morning Esther struggled
in sideways rain to feed the chickens.
As she hung her wet coat by the stove, a loud
bang came from the front of the house.

Her mother was busy feeding the baby.
Esther understood well that it was her job
to see to the problem, and Mother Bessie
would want her to be quick about it.

As she cautiously felt her way
into the hallway, another bang, this time
from behind the closed parlor door.

Children were not allowed in the parlor.
Esther had never entered it, and was
not at all sure she wanted to.

But slowly she turned the wooden knob,
opened the door a few inches. A queer light
spilled across the dark carpet onto her feet.

Curious now, she pushed the door farther open,
took a careful step and walked into the room.

An oak cabinet sat soberly against one wall,
illuminated by a gauzy window, its loose shutter
banging once more in the wind.

Esther continued closer to the cabinet
until her breath fogged its glass doors.
Inside were a blue and white teapot, two
crystal goblets, a porcelain shepherd,
and one plump sheep.

She wanted to touch the sheep, to see
closely its tiny face, the shepherd's
hand holding his staff.

Whatever are you doing, child? Bessie asked
sharply from the doorway.

Esther flooded with shame.
Surely a wicked, disobedient girl, she
stepped back and cast down her eyes.

There on the lowest shelf was a row
of books, each letter of the alphabet
in gold along their spines.

Mother! Esther said breathlessly. *Mother, look!*

Bessie's long, equine face darkened
in the gloom. She shushed Esther
hard and told her to never again
speak of them, to anyone.

Esther stood motionless, hot tears
welling. Bessie approached her
and took her gently by the shoulders,
looked into her dark eyes.

* * *

For a moment through her tears Esther
beheld the shimmering world, her mother
floating in that miraculous light. Then

the child descended, to where the fire
banked down deeply in her flared.

* * *

It would be a year before Esther dared
go back to the parlor. The books
were exactly as she'd remembered them.

She mouthed the letters, counted
the volumes—sixteen in all—then
dropped to her knees and reached for *A.*

From that day Esther spent every moment
she could, cross-legged in the dim light
behind the upholstered chair. Words
blossomed from every cranny of house
and barn, filled the corners of her tiny room.

Her head filled with sound—hieroglyph,
Himalayas, hoarfrost. *Helleborus argutifolius,*
a perennial found in Corsica, with palmate,
compound leaves—lory, an East Indian parrot
of the brush-tongued family *Trichoglossida—*

When she finished one volume, she
returned it and took down the next, until,
page by page, the whole set was done.
Then she started over.

* * *

The only other words in the house
were those Aaron commanded Esther
read aloud from the Bible. So she fashioned

a voice, as she had fashioned a child,
to serve him, to keep to herself
passages she so dearly loved.

                    Aaron could not read,
his teacher long ago having proclaimed him
a willful, stubborn boy. He'd follow
Esther's finger as she lifted the page, then
guided the one wing back to its body of words.

The other children fidgeted and quarreled,
asking finally if they could please go to bed.

Without breaking his gaze
Aaron would wave them away.

Though Esther ached from the day's work,
she read until Aaron grew sleepy, and, yawning
until his jaw cracked, sent her away as well,
too tired to demand anything more of her.

* * *

Aaron had no knowledge of the encyclopedia,
or that Bessie had bought the set from
a door-to-door salesman who appeared
one spring day at her garden gate.

He was a slight man with intense hazel eyes
so deeply set they gave him the appearance
of having fallen back into himself.

His voice, too,
seemed to come from that far place. *Good day, ma'am,*
he said, and cleared his throat. Bessie
was tending to the medicinal herbs,
cow bitter and boneset. She brightened

when she saw him—his waistcoat and striped
trousers, his black felt homburg—how he tucked
a stray hair under it with long, slender fingers.

She gathered her skirts, brushed off her knees,
and motioned him to come ahead. He nodded
shyly and stepped forward, startled by the gate
as it clacked shut behind him. He began
to speak, holding a large book in one hand,

pointing to it woodenly with the other—*This
staggering feat of humankind will bring vast intelligence*—
He took a deep breath and went on.

But Bessie was not listening—
Something sweet had stirred in her.
He had entered the kingdom of her garden, a place
only Esther was welcome, when
Bessie needed herbs for her cooking.

He had stepped in unknowing, as though this
were not the most unusual of gestures—a strange man
making his way gingerly through the tidy rows

of yarrow and feverfew toward a woman
so remote in her countenance she was rendered
all but invisible to a world she had long ago forsaken.

Yet the grace of his slender body, his full mouth
and perfect teeth, seemed to soothe the gall of her life.

This offer is only good for . . .

Yes, Bessie said quietly, interrupting the man,
whose gaze had drifted to the peonies
sprouting along the path where they stood.

What? he asked softly, turning to her, bewildered.

Into the silence came a meadowlark's watery call.

Yes, Bessie repeated.

* * *

Bessie hid the encyclopedia in the parlor,
knowing it was the one room
Aaron refused to enter.

At thirteen he'd seen his father laid out
in a parlor. All white and still,
he'd seemed vulnerable, defeated.

But it was the silence that had terrified him—
not so much a quiet as the opposite
of sound, the stale odor of it.

The night before, he'd hidden behind
the kitchen door and watched his mother
and grandmother bathe his father's body,
rail-thin from whatever it was killed him.

The wasting, Gram had said.

They stood on either side of the table where
his father lay on a clean sheet. Another
was folded across his lower torso.

From Aaron's view, his father's body fell
away from him, foreshortened.

Blackened footsoles obscured
the man's face, so the boy crept outside
and watched through the window.

The women spoke to each other so softly
Aaron could not make out the words, but their
voices were calm, almost joyful, as one, then
the other, wet her cloth in the porcelain basin,
wrung it out, and began. They worked in seamless,
continual motion, as if preparing a great feast.

But when they lifted the folded sheet, Aaron's
mother stopped and stepped back, arms
going limp at her sides. The wet cloth dropped
with a splat to the wood floor.

Aaron hated his father for dying, for leaving him
with these women. What did they know
about being a man?

* * *

Bessie had learned from her mother,
who had learned from Mennonite neighbors,
how to transform the prairie's unpredictable

harshness into flowers and vegetables,
fruit trees and climbing vines.

But one early summer, on the farm where
she grew to young womanhood, Bessie
took her mother's garden as her own.

It had been an unusually dry spring. Threat
of prairie fire held in the crackle underfoot.
The kitchen garden was the only green in sight.

The whole family had put to work clearing
a fire break to encircle the farm. Grimly,
her father turned the soil, his children alongside.

Grit got into her hair and eyes, and Bessie
thought to complain, but she knew better.

Then one night, while Father was away at auction
buying cattle, lightning struck the barn.
Fire began to kindle wider and higher.

Bessie woke to the fiery mouth
of her window, and when she stumbled to it,
she saw her mother, twenty rods west of the homestead,
where the barn was a growing knot of flame.

This must be a dream, Bessie thought.
Surely her mother was asleep across the hall—
Tennessee, too, tucked in on Father's side
of the bed whenever he was away.

The horses brought her to reason—their
god-awful, high-pitched squealing.

Her mother had opened the barn door
to let them out. The two bays and black
mare had taken off wild-eyed.

But her mother's favorite, the sorrel
with a tiny white star on his forehead,
reared up in panic, knocking her to the ground,
then ran back into the impossibly tall flames.

Fire caught the dry sod around her mother's
motionless body, for an instant forming a bright
outline of her dark silhouette.
                              Then she, too, was flame.

A blackness entered Bessie's heart, heavy
as a thing could be, but her mind focused suddenly
on the garden—its quiet, loamy coolness.

James had taken his little sisters' hands
and was hurrying down the stairs, Tenn and Pearl

trying to keep up, their nightgowns
billowing behind them.

Bessie guided them through the dooryard,
past the potato and asparagus beds,
the cherry saplings and peach orchard.

When they reached the flowerbeds and lilac
arbor, they stopped and huddled together,
surrounded by the deepening fragrance.

The house went up in fury, but the garden
went almost untouched.

James pumped water, as Father had taught him,
poured it bucket after bucket in circles
around his sisters, until, exhausted
he fell next to them and slept.

Neighbors came the next morning.
The men tied handkerchiefs
over their noses and mouths, buried
Bessie's mother, her sorrel alongside.

The women brought bread in colorful baskets,
stepping carefully among stinking cinders,
shaking their heads that such a thing could happen.

They begged Bessie to come home with them
and bring the other children. But Bessie and James,
Tennessee and Pearl stayed there four days
and nights, eating the spring vegetables
that grew around them, drinking from the well.

On the morning of the fifth day, Father
drove his wagon slowly up to what had been

the barn, turned north to the remains of the house.
He took in the rubble, the stone hearth
just as he had laid it, now in full sun,

then called out his wife's name.

* * *

A strange young man rode into town
looking for a few days' work.

Bessie was loading the wagon with kitchen staples
for the neighbor who had taken them in.
Aaron tipped his hat, his face sharp under it.

Bessie was a sturdy young woman, handsome
in her way. Boys had taken notice, but let her be,
in favor of the softer girls who smiled
even when the boys misbehaved.

Aaron saw her strong, straight back, her
steady face. She'd be his wife.

He don't deserve you, was all her father said.
Bessie believed it was true. But he had a wagon
and two good horses and was on his way west

to find a piece of land to farm so they'd have
what they needed and sell the rest.

He'd heard of a place some days out,
between two rivers, good corn crop,
house and barn mostly built.

She agreed to marry him, with one condition—

                                And so it was that
Bessie spent the next days gathering specimens
of each plant her mother had nurtured, filling
crates and buckets not already put to good use.

She wound burlap around the roots of saplings,
found the oleander overwintering in the cellar.

When the floor of the wagon was filled, she built
a frame above it and added another layer, then tied
the whole thing down with rope and twine.

As she and Aaron finally set out
they looked a sight—Aaron riding one horse
packed with his meager supplies, while

Bessie drove the wagon, mounded high—
bits of earth and leaves flying off
as she worked her way west.

* * *

On the second day of travel roads got sloppy from rain.
They camped early to get out of the wet, sheltered
under timber along the river. In the morning,
a herd of cattle nearly ran them through.

On the third day they stopped for a meal
at a man's house by the name of Six, Reverend Six.
The Reverend smiled when he saw the wagon.

Movers like Aaron and Bessie were welcome
to take a meal with folks along the way.
Firewood was stacked free along the road.

The prairie was broken and rough.
Next morning they crossed a good-sized creek
called Pumpkin. Their farm was not far.

* * *

But the first years revealed that Aaron had no
knack for farming. It was not that he
was lazy or weak or not smart enough.

He was a man who guessed wrong—

when to plant, when to harvest.
He let the wheat stand in shock until
it rained hard the day he was to thresh.

Nor was he good with the animals. Horses
agitated when he came near and pawed the ground.
Cattle scuttled, and the one bull
looked for something to butt.

At first Bessie felt sorry for him.
But he grew cruel and hard. Nothing and no one
pleased him. Soon enough she understood
that her husband was provoked not by some
demon, but a brutish, covetous hunger,

an appetite so unforgiving no food or smoke
or drink would satisfy. He ate only to quell his gut,
but the emptiness never left him.

She had grasped early on the depth of Aaron's
misery. Once, before they were married, he
kissed her so hard he drew blood on her lip,

would not loosen himself though she yipped
in pain. When finally she was able to break free—
his mouth smeared—he bristled like an animal

challenged for its kill. She knew
never to cross him again.

* * *

The wheat and oats stood in the shock,
pastures were lush and green. One day
a great glistening cloud gathered overhead
and as night fell it began to descend
in legions upon the land.

Locusts in such abundance they blanketed
every last parcel of the visible world
in writhing, terrible hunger.
They hit the house as loud as hail.
Tree limbs snapped from the weight.

What had been the rasping and whirring
of a billion insects approaching turned
to a thrumming cacophony. Listen more closely—
hear the mewl of lust and ardor,
satiety, utter and pitiless.

In two days they had eaten the landscape
back to winter, leveled the good crop.
They devoured every plant, leaf, and twig,
ate onions from the inside out, leaving

the skins intact, then headed into
the barns and houses to eat every scrap
of wood and cloth and kitchen staple—everything
their jaws could break, their guts digest.

Men tied string around the ankles of their trousers
to keep the creatures from crawling up their legs.
The cows went mad with no way to defend
against the invasion of ears and nose.

Water from streams and wells and ponds
was so fouled it was undrinkable, even for livestock.
Bloated hogs and chickens that had fed on them
were inedible, their meat blighted.

In the end, naked saw blades and pitchforks
littered the yard, their hafts eaten clean off.
                    Hard evidence.

Garden

The gods, who can only count to nine
Cling to their perches and, head under wing,
Sleep. They've pulled up the ladder.

—Robert Marteau, *Salamander*

The day Esther was born dawned orange
and gold. As honey light spilled onto the prairie,
Aaron got busy greasing his hardened boots
with hot tallow, stomped his sore feet into them,
startling the chickens clear across the yard.

Bessie's swelled belly was impossibly large,
yet she kept to her chores, which
she did not find disagreeable.

She'd made biscuits and sausage gravy
for breakfast, and while Aaron ate, she
strained away the morning's milk, put the cows
out to pasture. After she hung the day's
wash, she swept the dooryard.

The morning grew warm and breezy. Bessie
tended to her kitchen, wiped the table down,
straightened the chairs.

                    The child would sit there,
she imagined, *right there*—surely it would be
a girl—and paused as she saw her, her little legs
swinging, not long enough to reach the floor.

Outside, dark clouds were gathering, but
Bessie took no notice, until the sky
out the kitchen window turned queasy green.

Above the hydrangea a riot of moths
rose in the heat. A digger wasp drowsed on the sill,
folded its hinged, transparent wings.

Then everything went still.

One cloud flattened and spread over the western
pasture, and from its base lowered to the earth
a bright finger, backlit by a brighter sun, and wind

that soon lifted the barn roof and set it down
whole in a field a mile across town.

Nothing escaped Aaron's dominion.
When the storm passed he searched for the roof—
which looked oddly perfect where it lay,

as though the barn had sunk suddenly
to its rafters in that sweet corn, surrounded
by windrows of hedge apples.

When Aaron found the roof, he took it apart
board by board, with a plunderer's
imprecision—hauled it back by wagonloads
to the land he called his.

When he returned home that night
with the first load, he brushed the horse,
gave her a pail of feed. The sun had just set
behind the western rise, but the house was still dark.

Aaron opened the kitchen door and found Bessie
sitting hunched over the table, and when
she looked up, her pale face seemed
untethered in the gloaming.

Aaron fetched the neighbor, and soon enough
the infant girl lay wide-eyed beside her sleeping
mother, tiny fingers fluttering like the gills of a fish.

* * *

As Aaron grew more restless and cold-hearted,
Bessie seemed to grow taller, straighter
in the green field of a familiar task, when
her spirit entered that other place
not tainted with human breath or woe.

What others knew as the tyranny of farm life
Bessie welcomed. Her garden above all,
the sweet-sour minglings and rustlings.

Her mother's garden had followed a quincunx
pattern—five sections, four squared, one in the center.

But as she and Aaron neared the farm
that first day, Bessie saw instantly the place
where she would plant—

a graceful sweep of earth on the south side
of the house. It would get a full day's sun,
and was shaped like a leaf, tapering between
two hawthorns, west toward the prairie.

A stone path would follow the main vein
of the leaf, smaller paths branching off.

Bessie worked to prepare the ground
until her hands bled. Aaron was no help.
He thought she was a fool and said so.

Within a week Bessie got the plants in the ground,
and as she saw the leaf pattern emerge, she
stood back and wept. The next morning Aaron cut

through the garden to lessen his journey from
house to barn, walked right over what she had
planted, grinding his feet as he went.

She built a fence, dug up thorny pyracantha
from the bank of the stream.

Finally Aaron left the garden alone.

She planted caster beans to repel moles,
borage and marigolds to ward off

tomato worms and wild rabbits. She planted
basil around the kitchen porch for mosquitoes
and flies, garlic alongside onions to deter mice.

Soon the garden was thriving and lush, humming
with bees and butterflies.

                    The grapevine
survived, though did not leaf out the first year,
did not bear fruit until the next.

Bessie had built an arbor, so when
the grapes came, they had room to grow.

That year the peach trees matured,
their fruit plentiful, white, and sweet.

* * *

Bessie had become the land, had taken on
its contours, its harsh beauty.

At the clothesline, she bent to the task
of hollowing the basket, shook the clothes out
hard, raised them to the fields of air.

Behind her, the fierce loneliness
of prairie stretched as far as her life.

Mornings at the soapstone sink, she gazed
out at the wind raking the buffalo grass,

the crape myrtle that each summer
spread its brilliance.

                       One day, she promised
Esther, *one day I'm going to lay myself
under that tree and never get up.*

* * *

Aaron was not a smiling man, nor one
who talked more than he had to. Neither
was he a thinking man, a patient man.

But when Esther learned to walk
and toddled after him like a duckling—
from the infirmity of his conscience—came

a kind of tolerance, which on the surface
might have seemed like affection. But Aaron
was incapable of such charity.

When she squealed with delight
at his presence, he gleaned from her adoration
merely a mirror image of the man
he thought himself to be—powerful
and righteous, in total control.

He began to take her wherever he went,
made a little harness so that she would
not fall from the wagon.

William was born, and Lela. Aaron
wanted nothing to do with them.

Bessie was busy now with three children
and all that the farm demanded. Even the distant
relationship she and Aaron shared was gone.

As Esther began to pull away, he became
scornful of her small child's enthusiasms
if they did not include him.

Stern and overbearing, he'd command her
to go without supper.

Who had a better right than a father
to make his child behave as he pleased?

The need to hurt burst into his veins,
as if some sudden, deadly disease
had taken hold of him.

Hurt was all he really knew, and it had
waited sullenly in the shadows—

Then one evening, when Esther was four years
and three months, he reached under her
nightdress and broke her.

* * *

This land once belonged to the Osage, until
the treaty of Drum Creek opened a narrow strip
along the eastern side to settlement.

That year the first settler was a Negro, whose
master had once cracked the boy's back with a shovel.
Louis Scott summoned his nerve and ten dollars

to secure his claim. And it was in this valley—
rich bottom land and timber belts of hackberry,
hickory, and oak—that a slave finally broke free.

* * *

Aaron blamed the horses, or the weather.
The farm was too big, the river too wide.

Too many children when food was scarce,
too few when the work became demanding.

So he made a plan to go farther west, though
the frontier had closed decades before.

He'd go to the mountains where there
was still work logging the big pines.
It was illegal to log in those mountains, but
Aaron didn't care. They made him foreman.

The work was temporary, and would be
over by fall, and he could return, he assured
Bessie, with more money than she'd ever seen.
But Aaron had no intention of returning.

He chose Esther to go with him. Esther,
who'd grown tall and strong, who wore
her black hair wound around her head.

Rumor was that Osage poisoned his bloodline
and Esther looked every inch an Indian.
But Aaron would not hear of it.

She's a Kansan, he'd say, *through and through.*

Esther—the child who lived inside her head,
who knew things her father could not fathom.

At fifteen, she'd be good company, he said.

* * *

When Aaron announced his plan, Bessie
took to her room like a storm heading east,
through the scumbled throat of the house,

the dark stairway with its somber
framed faces in their starched collars, each face
saying, *She is his. He has bespoken her.*

                    That night, when the house
was still and Aaron's breathing went deep,
she fetched from the linen closet the torn
remains of the blouse she'd worn
on her wedding day, sat with it in the darkened
kitchen, her hands folded in her lap.

Bessie had never been touched by a man
before Aaron. When she'd hesitated,
he'd held her down and ripped her blouse

from the neck, exposing her breasts and belly,
the buttons she had so carefully sewn
down the front popping in every direction.

Frightened and ashamed, she gave in.
He took her then with vulgar disregard,
and when he was done, he rolled off her,
one arm flung over her chest.

Soon he was inside some hard dream, his fists
                    clenching and unclenching.

She lay there, the weight of his arm becoming
unbearable, until with a snort, he turned over.

During their first long year of marriage,
she'd take out the ivory cloth and feel again
Aaron's flinty hand over her mouth.

After a time, she tried to let it all go—hid
the blouse behind the ironed sheets.

* * *

On that vast intelligence of prairie, a child
had waved her slender arms—beckoning,

foundering—Time fell straight down,
no matter the prayer. What was there to learn
from such a heavy thing—a father
visiting misery on his own child?

What would make a child not run
from such misery? And if the child ran, what evil
would pull up the ladder?

* * *

Sunup, as Esther packed last things into
the satchel—undergarments, the tortoiseshell
brush Aunt Tenn had promised her—her mother

knocked and slowly entered the room,
tears collecting along her lip. Surprised
by her mother's presence, Esther fell quiet.

    Hurry up, for chrissake,
Aaron hollered up from the kitchen.

Big River

Agamemnon: *There is another journey you must take—*
And you will not forget your father there.

—Euripides, *Iphigenia in Aulis*

Esther paused on the gangway
to catch her breath. She set her bags down
to wave one last time to her mother.

But Bessie was already headed back
to the farm, the empty dray rattling,
the horse's brindled flanks and black tail
dwindling in the dawn light.

The train smelled of boot polish and onions.
Esther followed Aaron through car after car
but it was no use.

Passengers from Eureka Springs
and Fort Smith and all the way from
St. Louis filled every seat and spilled
noisily into the aisles.

When they reached the rear of the last
coach Aaron turned and motioned Esther
to step aside, then moved ahead of her
to begin again through the cars.

He poked his face excitedly over the shoulder
of a passenger holding on to the baggage rack
at what seemed an empty seat.

Aaron and the man swayed in unison
as the train took a curve. A mother
bending to lace her child's shoe

sat back up, straightened her hat.
Aaron swore softly and pushed on.
Esther felt a sudden rush of sadness

at the sight of him, smaller somehow,
his head down and shoulders drawn in
like an animal burrowing its way to shelter.

* * *

A mother holding a crying infant
stood abruptly as the train pulled in

to Independence, and as she guided
the head of a toddler into the aisle,
passengers rushed for the emptied seats.

But Aaron had noticed the woman
gathering her belongings, and had pardoned
himself into position, so that before
she rose fully, to shift the baby in her arms,
he heaved himself behind her, slapped his hat
down on the window seat, and collapsed

into the other, one leg still in the aisle.
The woman sniffed her disapproval,
pulled the child to her skirts.

Esther settled into the seat Aaron had
commandeered, too embarrassed to look up
until they reached Independence.

As several passengers stood to gather
their belongings, she unbuttoned her collar
and sat back exhausted.

* * *

At Wichita the creaking of brakes
gave way to excited squeals. A passel
of ragtag children on the platform

waved and hollered as the train slowed
but did not stop.

                    Newton, and another
exchange of passengers, and finally the train
headed west. Esther's eyes grew heavy

as she took in one sorry acre after another.
Here and there a farm sat defiantly,

outbuildings dotting the prairie as if
thrown by some dry explosion, and there
they stayed, stuck in the thrall of consequence.

* * *

Piled two storeys high along the tracks
leaving town were bleached buffalo
bones, a mountain of them.

Freighted to the big cities, the bones
were made into combs and buttons,
ground into fertilizer. Once a herd

could stretch for twenty-five miles, four
million strong. A single mass of buffalo.

Now there wasn't a buffalo alive on the plains,
except maybe stuffed in a museum somewhere
where no buffalo ever roamed.

* * *

Esther pretended to inspect the hem
of her shirtwaist so as not to see Aaron

fill his pipe, pack the tobacco down
with his thick thumb, so she did not know

the train had approached the Arkansas
with its wrought-iron bowstring bridge,
trusses that cut the sky into bright triangles.

As the train mounted the bridge, the rhythmic
clacking grew hollow. Vertical thrusts
leapt suddenly, casting deep shadows

on Esther's hands, and when in alarm
she raised her head, the sleepy passengers,

the painted linoleum ceiling, and the beveled
transom pulsed in perfect sequence.

                    Out the window,
a river meandered beyond the chaos.

* * *

Esther had seen a river once before.
Early one morning Aaron had ordered Bessie
to the feed store in Independence

and, while she was at it, to pick up
a box of ten-penny nails.

Curled up in the front parlor,
Esther overheard them. Before
the rest of the family had yawned awake,

she had found her way in the dark
to the kerosene lamp, the chair
at the far end of the room, where
the encyclopedia sat neatly on its shelf.

Today she was deep into the *M*'s. In Mexico,
she learned, all the people are lazy
and sleep much of the day away.

                       Siesta,
whispered Esther, and imagined whole
villages asleep in their beds while the hens
got loose from the henhouse.

What's the matter with the store in town?
Bessie demanded. Esther could hear
the turn in her mother's voice.

Aaron did not reply. Esther knew
he'd be lighting his morning pipe. She
could hear him strike the match

on the iron stove, could hear
from down the long hall the flame
burst—could feel the heat even as she sat
as small as she could make herself.

Esther knew, too, what her father planned
while Mother Bessie was away, why
he was sending her to town.

She rose quickly, placed the volume
carefully between *L* and *N*, and hurried
up the front stairs to her attic room.

Through her dormered window she saw
Aaron head toward the wagon he'd hitched
and tied to the gate of the kitchen garden,

where Bessie now stood, arms stiff at her sides,
among paperwhites and narcissus
in early show along the privet hedge.

Esther dressed quickly, laced up
her boots, and descended the back stairway

as her father methodically checked the traces
and hames, tightened the horse's girth.

When he turned to meet Bessie's
dour face, Esther met his eyes instead
                                    and seized the reins.

Where do you think you're going, girl? Aaron snarled,
stepping back. But Esther had already mounted
the wagon, felt the mare's delicate mouth

respond from the bit down the length of the leather.
Before Aaron could stop her she ordered the horse   *Ride!*

She knew Independence was west, so drove
hard away from the rising sun
until she came to a wide river, wildness

she could not yet fathom, a ribbon
of copper green moving so swiftly behind
a stand of cottonwood that for an instant

it looked to the girl as if the trees were moving
while the river stood still.
                                    She wondered
where in the world all that water came from,

then turned the wagon around
and headed back home.

* * *

The land brooded with sad farms, barley
just taking hold that would not survive
the drought or the merciless wind,

and beyond the barley grew sorghum,
as far as the eye could see, and what land
did not support a crop suffered buffalo grass,

and prairie dogs the farmers called fury
weeds, busy with their miserable lives.

Esther could not have known while
she dozed—just one of many on this train
traveling in regimental discomfort, folks

who would die working the land
and be buried there—that beneath them,

the great continent of Pangaea was once
split by a vast inland sea, where
winged lizards and giant sharks

and turtles twice the size of an ox
held sway, and long-necked plesiosaurs

with great oar-like paddles prowled
alongside graceful, serpentine
predators forty-five feet, twenty tons—

where she now stirred and nearly
wakened from her dream of mountains,

trillions of miniscule organisms sank
to sea bottom, their delicate carcasses
forming the chalk hills and limestone

quarries and shale beds that shaped
this prairie—what this girl understood
as flat, unchanging, was in fact the slow

rumination of what had always been,
shifting without notice, the forcemeat
of time on all things.

* * *

Aaron had unfolded the map
and struggled to set it flat enough to read,
but the best he could do left two hills
where his knees bent under it.

Esther sat very still as she always did
if it fell to her to be nearest him
when he was vexed.

Here! We must be here! Aaron blurted
to no one in particular. Startled
out of her stillness, Esther followed

her father's gaze to one of the hills
where his finger jabbed at a black dot
beside a thin blue line.

She had seen maps in the encyclopedia,
maps of Africa, of mountains in South America,
the whole British Empire. Never
had she seen a map of Kansas.

Where did we start, Father? Esther asked.
But Aaron was at it again, trying
to smooth the paper, and paid no attention.

So she leaned in and saw that he had circled
Montgomery County, where the farm sat
heavy on the land, where Bessie's brooding

countenance brightened as she worked
in the kitchen garden, its precise rows
of potatoes, sugar beets to feed the hens.

Esther conjured the snap peas and kale
near the tidy bed of verbena, her mother
bending to harvest thyme and marjoram,

their lingering fragrance.

Then the girl looked up toward her attic room
and saw herself there at the window,
gazing out beyond the barn.

She was thinner than she'd imagined
herself to be, in that life, just days ago, but
she'd thought her mouth to be a grim slash
across her face.
                And it was.

The smell of fried chicken brought her back
to the train, to the family across the aisle

noisily opening their box lunches,
and to Aaron, still fingering the map.

Disquiet settled in her stomach.
Everywhere she had ever been in her life
was within the distance of the width
of her father's hand.

The Song of the Lark

The impeded stream is the one that sings.

—Wendell Berry

He sat across the aisle, part of the noisy
family eating their lunch—a boy, but
full grown, with a wide, easy face.

His mother handed him a biscuit
and a butter knife, then opened a crock
of strawberry jam and offered it. The boy's

face brightened as he dipped into the crock
and spread the jam carefully just to the edge
of the biscuit and brought it hungrily to his mouth.

Esther had never seen such tenderness.

He turned to her as if she had said something
and she quickly lowered her eyes.

                    Where're you from?
the boy asked, leaning into the aisle a bit,
brushing crumbs from his lap. Esther

felt her face redden. She wanted to tell him
how much she despised her father, how ashamed
she was for never having seen a mountain.

Instead she said nothing, avoided his eyes.
After a time the boy sat back and crossed his arms.

The conductor steadied himself on the seat backs
as he made his way through the car.
                              Kinsley! Kinsley next stop!

The family clamored into the aisle, the boy
last, as the train pulled into the station.

He looked back at Esther, opened his mouth
to speak, seemed to think better of it,
then followed the others.

                    * * *

A loneliness settled upon Esther as the boy
turned to leave. A kind of luminous
sadness spread to every part of her, made her

suddenly aware of her feet bound
by thick stockings and ill-fitting shoes, the collar
of her shirtwaist stiff against her neck—awake

to the soft boundaries of her body giving way,
her skin, as it held her, transforming
cell by cell into what surrounded her—

the mustiness of the crowded train, muffled
voices, the constant drone of the engine—

until the terrifying exquisite otherness
of the world washed over her, inside her,
and, though barely perceptible,
played on her lips.

* * *

She stayed that way for a long while,
as if someone were speaking to her,

and she, in rapt attention, listened, as if
nothing would matter ever again—

until something on the seat where the boy
had been sitting brought her back—a book.

She looked around to see if anyone else
had noticed, then retrieved it. On the dark blue
cover, inside a rectangle of gold, was the title—

The Song of the Lark—and below that,
three dots of gold, and then *W. S. Cather.*

On the first page—
> *It was a wond'rous lovely storm that drove me!*—

and on the next—

On uplands,
At morning,
The world was young, the winds were free;
A garden fair,
In that blue desert air,
Its guest invited me to be.

She leafed through the book,
then opened it at random.

She wandered for a long while about the sand ridges, picking up
crystals and looking into the yellow prickly pear blossoms with their
thousand stamens. She looked at the sand hills until she wished she
were a sand hill.

A strange heat entered Esther, sweetbitter
and foreign—and she longed for it to stay, but just then
Aaron blinked awake.

Look, Father, she said,
feigning excitement, and pointed
with her right hand toward the window.
                    We're nearing Dodge!

His eyes followed sleepily and she buried the book
with her left hand, deep in her satchel.

* * *

*Dodge was once a cow town, the biggest
and busiest in the west. A herd of longhorns
might have been driven here all the way
from the Texas panhandle.*

*They'd be fattened up spring and summer,
then brought to the nearest railhead,
sold to brokers back East.*

*But the great cattle drives were over —
barbed wire brought an end to that.*

*What cattle there were grazed in clumps
along the soil-rich banks of the river,
and the bulk of the land was given over
to winter wheat, Turkey Red, out there
beyond what Esther could see, vast*

*stretches, the wind combing some great head
of hair, whose face would never turn toward the sun.*

*Sodbusters, the farmers called themselves.
All day they broke the spine of the earth —
driving their new machines across the prairie's*

*fragile surface. What were once wild expanses
of native grass were turned to oceans of grain. Now,
as spring spread its warmth, the winter crop*

matured toward harvest. Columns of dark
smoke soon would appear all over the uplands,
where threshing crews, arriving at dawn,

would begin their long day—feeding
the stationary steam engine, its flywheel
attached to the thresher's by a wide leather belt,
feeding, too, the thresher's mouth with shocks
of wheat, to separate hay from chaff.

* * *

I'm not going in any fancy hotel with you
just to look, Aaron announced, as they stood
on the gangway waiting for a full stop.

When at last the screeching brakes fell silent,
he bounded down the steep steps
and headed across the tracks for town.

If you go in there, he yelled over his shoulder,
don't you go talking to any strangers.

But by now Esther's legs were leaden
and her hands felt clumsy, as though she were
wearing thick mittens. She tried to step aside
but instead her knees locked as passengers

squeezed around her. *I'm sorry*, she said,
sorry, to each one, her head perceiving
the awkwardness, but her body fixed in space.

She thought of the boy she would never see again—
how easily he had moved through the train,
had disappeared for a moment and appeared
again on the platform—how he had waved to her.

She took each downward step carefully,
a flutter in her stomach at the thought
of a strange place. Alone.

She reached the landing and filled her lungs,
looking back at Aaron only once
as he gingerly picked his way across
the mass of converging rails in the busy hub
Dodge had become, lifting his legs
to clear the height of each rail.

He seemed to Esther like a child playing
marching band, his gait exaggerated, his
body focused only on the next step.

A train crossed slowly between them, blocking
her father from view. Esther felt suddenly sick.
What if he didn't come back?

* * *

The station was a long dark brick building
with a sign in gold lettering: *A Harvey House.*

Esther had heard about the Harvey Girls,
and wanted to see for herself how they carried
a whole tray of meals and never spilled a drop, fed
a whole train full of people in fifteen minutes.

The lobby was cool and fragrant. She recognized
tobacco, but not the kind Aaron smoked
in his horrid pipe. This smelled of fruit
and earth. It was on her hands, in her hair.

Leather armchairs were placed throughout
the room, potted ferns filled the spaces between.
Milky globes suspended from the ceiling
lit up suddenly—someone had turned the switch
as the prairie darkened.

From the dining room, the tink of cutlery.

She followed the others through the lobby
and the big dining room doors, then fell back
into a shadow behind one door to watch.

Hungry passengers sat hurriedly at the immaculate
tables, each covered with imported linen, set
with fine china, crystal, and silverware.
In the center fresh fruit and Roquefort
cheese and a cut-glass pitcher.

Brightly starched and smiling, two Harvey Girls
appeared at each table, one behind the other,
the first to take drink orders, the second
to fill the glass with milk or iced tea, taking
her cue from where the first placed the glass.

English pea soup au gratin in a proper crock
was served next. The Harvey Girls rhythmically
circled the tables, bending gracefully to each request,
and when the last guest put down his fork, the Girls
swept the tables clean of plates and served
homemade peach pie and New York ice cream.

Esther hadn't realized how hungry she was.
She and Aaron had eaten their supper long before
Dodge, from the basket Bessie had packed.
She eyed a shiny apple and her mouth ran wet
at the thought of biting into it.

The train whistled to call the passengers back,
and as the last of them filed noisily out the door,
one Harvey Girl stepped forward.

She was a few years older than Esther, and as tall,
her dark hair swept up onto her head with a ribbon.
Wisps had escaped and fallen in ringlets at the nape
of her neck and over her blue-white collar.

Her forehead and upper lip were moist.
She held a napkin, its four corners tied into a pouch.
There was a radiance about her that was unsettling
and as she moved closer Esther caught the loamy,
musky sweetness of skin.

Here, she said, handing the napkin to Esther. *Take this.*

As Esther rushed for the train she felt a round
heaviness through the cloth, and something
soft too. An unfamiliar odor escaped as she
peeled back one corner, alarming yet savory.
There, tucked in with an apple was the strange
cheese, dark green lacing its creamy body.

* * *

Esther found Aaron's seat empty, then
spotted him out the window at the far edge
of the rail hub, as he began his way back.
He sank his right hand into his pocket as if
he were returning a sword to its scabbard.

Aaron was a graceless man, but this gesture,
so blindly self-assured, so free of guile, raised
him for that brief moment into the realm
of better men, fathers who don't hurt
their children, who might even love them.

The train whistle brought Aaron to reason,
and soon he was running, high-stepping forward
to clear the tracks, both arms flailing. Esther
could not bear to watch and turned away.

* * *

The big river stayed mostly in sight now.
Gone, the man-high grasses—
big bluestem, prairie oats, Indian grass—
save along draws and valleys.

Gone the wild fescue of the rich
eastern woodlands, where hedgerows
of Osage orange, dogwood,
and persimmon offered nesting
for northern bobwhite quail.
The grove of walnut trees
was folded into memory.

This was sandsage prairie, buffalo
grass, drop seed covering the sandhills,
and, in the river lowlands, fine top—
bunched, short grasses, good for grazing.

This was the land of bitterweed,
yellow nut grass and sagebrush, sweet
sand verbena flowering at dusk, its
calyx corolla-like blossoms
whitest in moonlight—

a semi-arid steppe, where wind
had driven settlers mad, and the chinook
rendered everything unpredictable.
Pronghorns thrived in the harshness
of these high plains; at four days old
they could outrun a man.

* * *

The night before Esther and her father
left the farm, Aunt Tennessee had told Esther
how she'd heard of a woman who'd settled
with her family in the uplands—*where*

you'll be passing through, she'd said solemnly,
and leaned in close to touch Esther's knee.

Tennessee was large and broad-shouldered,
able to do the work of a man, but her voice
was soft and small, full of a child's wonder,
and when she spoke, a story came forth.

The woman was born east—east, Tenn
would say again, *where I myself was born
and forevermore dream of returning.*

Then she closed her eyes, as if
she were right there in that landscape,
trees and flowers, where someone once knew
someone who had seen the ocean.

*So surrounded was this woman
by boundless solitude*, Tenn continued quietly,
her loneliness blossomed to need—so hungry

*was she for the sight of trees, she put her arms
around the one cottonwood in the county,
and would not let it go.*

* * *

Settlers must have believed the wind
was born here, thought Esther, with no
beginning, no end to it. She mourned
the landscape she had left. Still,

something in the dryness, the urgency
of sunset drawn clean and hard
along the horizon, took her heart.

She imagined the woman out there—
standing alone against the wind, her feet
disappearing in a swale of gray-green—

when something white appeared on the horizon—
a bit of fluff, a cloud, she thought, and then
a few more emerged farther south.

                              Look! someone shrieked,
You can see the mountains!

A shiver of excitement rippled
audibly through the train.

From her aisle seat, Esther leaned toward
the window, careful not to touch Aaron,
whose head had flopped back,
his mouth agape in a snore,

but all she could see were those clouds.
Could it be? she thought.
Why, they're nothing at all.

And just as surely as passengers
ignited in wonder, they settled back into
the numbing monotony of travel,

someone's attention now and again
drawn away from her needlework, whose
gaze drifted toward the window, then
returned inward to her task.

But no task could calm Esther.
No embroidery or cross stitch or crewel,
no smocking or hemming or tacking
could make her sit still, make her
take her eyes off the mirage of white
along the horizon growing infinitesimally
as dusk flooded the prairie.

Not the *American Magazine* she'd
bought with her own money at the depot
at Dodge, and smiled when she thought how
wasteful Aaron would think the purchase.

Not even the story she was slowly entering,
about a girl whose name meant *gift of god,*
who explored the very landscape
through which Esther now sped—
and who dreamed of more.

* * *

When her father had come at her
with his terrible hardness, Esther
sometimes would not obey. She'd close herself up
tight and small, a fist of a girl.

                    Once she laughed,
and heard herself, as if she were some other
child amused by a playmate. Aaron ran from the bed,
the grommets of his suspenders clacking.

But Esther feared one thing: the dark.
And it was dark on the prairie that night,
the kind of dark that gulped the world down

whole—the train rushing its hard body
into starlessness. All night, its one note.

By the light of the single lamp turned low
Esther saw her head and shoulders floating
gauzily in the black frame of the window, worry

streaking her face. She tried not to, but sat
forward to see herself again, and as she turned,
her face disappeared. She looked
for her hands, but they, too, were gone.

She fell through waves of sound,
then no sound.

                    Blasted lamp! someone swore,

then a scuffle. When they'd relit the lamp
and dimness returned, Esther was sitting
as she had been, her face held captive
in the frame, but her eyes had softened.

She'd come back. She was Esther Arena Kennedy,
sixteen in August, and the mountains
were waiting for her.

* * *

Aaron filled his pipe, drew deeply
to get the bowl lit, settled back
and crossed one leg over the other.

He went far away then, to a place
Esther could only imagine, but was
always grateful for. He lingered

for those moments, shrouded
in his foul-smelling smoke—but
just as Esther entered her own place

apart, he turned abruptly, formed a perfect *O*
with his lips, and blew a smoke ring
into the air between them that

grew to the size of a dinner plate.

When we get there, girl, you won't be
with anyone but me. You hear?
                              Esther nodded.

* * *

Aaron's bitterness grew over the one thing
he could not control—Esther's mind—how
a curious softness had come gradually

over her face and taken her away from him.
She'd turned ever so slowly inward
and nothing he did could get her back.

As they crossed the high plains together,
characters strange and wonderful
lived now inside her, too. Aaron could not
own this, could not even know it.

* * *

As the sun lifted the prairie into light,
the mountains slowly raised their white arms.

By the time the train entered La Junta
Aaron had fallen back to sleep.
When it jerked to a stop and the brakes

hissed, his breathing stayed deep.
His eyes fluttered once, then closed.

Esther put away her needlework, tucked
the book carefully back into her satchel,
and stowed it under her seat.

On the platform the air was dry and smelled
of locomotive. She was afraid to look west, afraid
the mountains had gone away.

But there they were, familiar somehow, as if
they'd been outside her attic window, always,

beyond the far field of Indian grass
and bluestem, at the edge of her world.

* * *

The boarding house was set back from the street—
a grand Victorian built for some baron who'd
gotten rich off the mines at Cripple Creek.

Small orchards of carefully pruned crabapple
and plum flanked the stone path to the front door.
Esther was gripped with sadness.

How Bessie would love this yard—quiet,
thoughtfully designed, everything in its place.

.

The proprietor, a stout woman with startling
blue eyes, greeted them coolly.

Staying two nights?

Yes, ma'am, Aaron answered, oddly polite.

Will you want time at the springs?

No, he answered, with growing impatience.

You're in number seven, she said, gesturing
to the stairs, then handed Aaron a key.

You'll be needing another bed then?

Hoisting his trousers, Aaron said nothing
and strode past her. Esther avoided her gaze
and hurried behind him.

The room faced the street, with a large bay window.
Dark molding framed pink rose wallpaper.
The toilet was at the end of the long hall.

Aaron had planned their first day carefully.
While he met with the man who owned the camp,
Esther would wait for him.

She watched Aaron turn the corner
into town, then looked around her. Everything
was her father—his smell, his bed.

A restlessness marshaled in her as she
navigated the lacy canyon of that room.

She took the stairs two at a time, flung
the front door wide. The air was crisp,
the light—different from Kansas somehow.
For this only she hesitated— then ran

down the path. A tram rumbled
to a stop on the street. The driver looked
puzzled, as if he'd never seen a girl
running for her life. Without breaking
stride Esther stepped on.

She searched her pockets for a nickel
and handed it to the man, who clicked it
routinely into his coin changer.

The brass overhead rail was cool in her hand.
As the driver shifted into gear, Esther
planted her feet wider for balance.

Herefords bunched and thinned down
the main street, surrounding a horse-drawn
sprinkler wagon. Esther felt sorry for the man
driving the wagon and the poor spooked horse,
its eyes wild and piercing in all that confusion.

When someone opened the sash, a warm wind
stroked her face. Esther relaxed her jaw,
took a deep breath.

* * *

It hadn't mattered where the tram was going,
and after a bit, it slowed and stopped
as a tiny station came into view. On the track
sat an odd little rail car, with a center cog
wheel like a clock's sprocket. It must be a toy,
Esther thought. Whatever is it for?

The car had big windows surrounding all sides.
Esther followed the other passengers and chose
a seat at the rear. The car jolted and began to climb.

She felt strangely calm as the station grew
smaller and smaller and the car lifted quickly
above it into the foothills of scrub oak
and piñon pine, meadows of Indian paintbrush.

The first boulder field came into view, scattered
as if the ruins an ancient city—like the one of waste

and confusion Isaiah warned would come to pass.
Esther had imagined it so clearly. But she felt
no wickedness here, no shame.

Farther up the mountain spread dense
woodlands of ponderosa pine. Mule deer
grazed in a grove of aspen. Soon, everything
began to compress from incessant wind and cold.

Bristlecone pine thrived along the tree line—stunted,
disfigured. Then, no trees at all, but ridge after ridge
of deep vertical slides marbled with snow.

Big-horned sheep maneuvered an outcropping.
Another turn of the track and an inaccessible wall
of peerless granite reared up, but the train
miraculously reached fourteen thousand feet—

Esther stepped out onto the broken rock. Snow
and soft hail surrounded her. As she walked,
the wind made its own silence, swallowing
even the crunch of her footsteps.

When it cleared she was nearing the edge
of the north face, from which a vast
amphitheater of rock plummeted.

She sensed she'd been there before, that
all this had happened to her already.

Then, a solitary, pink-tinged cloud a half-mile down
began to move across the abyss, and as it did,
a mass of cold air hit her with such sucking force
the skin on her neck pricked in terror. The cloud

lit up with bright bluish alarm, as a bolt
of lightning shot toward the mountain's base—
a lilac haze emerged then from below—rain
for the villagers eating their noon meal.

She looked east, where the prairie unfolded,
where morning had risen and each day
of her life had begun. A tawny carpet
stretched to the horizon and over.

All she'd ever known
was out there somewhere.

* * *

Esther lingered a while, the sun
at her back, her shadow lowering its dark cape
over feldspar and lichen, toward home.

In spring the Tabeguache Utes once
moved their families into the lushness
of the high basins to hunt buffalo.

Now,
the lakes and basins, the bristlecone
in their magnificent survival—even the mountains
were the white man's.

* * *

Though it was past supper when she reached
to the boarding house, Esther felt no hunger.

Aaron was sitting in the dark, a silhouette
floating in the window bay, his hat

still on his head. He'd pulled a chair up
to watch the street. On his lap

was the book he'd found in her satchel.

Where've you been? he demanded, not turning around.
His voice was hoarse, uneven.

Where the hell have you been?

Train

There are two gates of sleep.

—Virgil, *Aeneid*

What was not log and rubblestone was
hard-edged, the air clear and cold.

Twenty loggers worked the camp. Twenty
hungers found Esther, no matter how
she carved the slim time she had for herself.

And Aaron's gaze on her never let up,
even as he drove his men each morning
on the flatwagon out of sight—

                  Even then
she felt it—until finally she fell exhausted
into the hard bed he had fashioned for her,
next to the huge wood cook stove, whose
intolerable heat was entirely hers to feel.

* * *

Esther's realm was the kitchen
and she soon learned to let no one enter.

Supplies were brought to the side door.
She lugged the fifty-pound bags of flour
and sugar to the tilt-out bins and, with a great
heave, lifted them into place.

The bins were the sole convenience
in an otherwise stark chamber. But Esther
had grown to love the quiet.

Ice was hauled from Denver, and the icebox
sat squarely at the far end of the room,
away from the stove that crackled

and spit from well before dawn, when
Esther filled the firebox and worked

the dampers to get a good steady
heat for the morning's biscuits.

Molasses came in kegs, and when
each was done, Esther scraped up

the brown sugar that had bottom-settled
and kept it in a jar for herself.

* * *

While the other loggers pushed back
their chairs from the long plank table
and jostled into position toward

early morning light, Raymond, his first day
at the camp, had risen quietly, alone finally
in the rough-hewn room, to bring his

empty plate and mug to the kitchen
as his mother had taught him.

Esther sat facing away from him, peeling
a vat of potatoes for the noon meal.
This was her favorite time of day—

the men leaving for the mountain.
She could sing if she wanted.

She had unbuttoned her smock, let it
fall from her shoulders to expose her back

to cool air from the opened window.
Esther's skin was moist and flushed

and in that morning light the most
beautiful thing Raymond had ever seen.

He drew in a quick, sharp breath as if
wakened suddenly from deep slumber.

Esther turned, her mouth opening softly
in surprise, as Raymond's gaze

reached her. In that instant
her dark eyes took him in. He stood
tall and slender, with a shock of thick

auburn hair. His jaw was square and his back
straight, his hands large and clean.

An *Oh* was all Esther could muster, but no sound
came, as Raymond backed out the same door

he came in, still holding his soiled dishes.
A girl's forearm on the hottest summer day
was all he had ever had the pleasure to observe.

Now this. *This.*

* * *

Her horse was the closest thing to a friend
Esther had in those mountains.

They rode one morning along the hogback,
then moved west where the escarpment
leveled off, higher into the foothills.

Esther halted to rest,
let the paint drink from spring runoff meandering
through a meadow of greasewood and sage.

She tied him to a sapling, stroked
his long neck and withers, the base of his ear,

and down his silky cheek, all the while
crooning, *Good horse. There's a good horse.*

At the edge of the stream, Esther cupped water
and drank greedily, her reflection

rippling outward in perfect circles. Then something
moved on the opposite bank.

She stood up in surprise, shielding her eyes
from the sun to see what was there.

A man took shape in the haze.
Behind him a wide fringe of ponderosa pine
spread like enormous wings.

Raymond had been there first, had watched
Esther ride up to the stream and dismount, her paint
bow his head and nicker as Esther gentled him.

He'd wanted to shout hello when she first appeared
riding slowly through the sage, but thought
better of it. What if she didn't remember him?

But Esther did remember him—the delicious
startle and confusion that day in the kitchen,
a young man approaching her without
warning, wanting nothing from her.

When he'd stumbled out, she had quickly
refastened her smock and sat for a bit in the stillness.
She could feel his presence in the room,
closed her eyes and breathed him in.

Now, from across the stream she felt it—
and before she realized, she'd raised her hand
in greeting, and Raymond did the same.

He paused, then waded across the shallow water,
leading his own horse behind him. His shadow
reached her before him, and the fragrant
complexity of leather and horse, a man's clean
sweat, meadow of wild onion and prickly pear.

I'm sorry if I frightened you, ma'am, Raymond said,
stepping carefully toward her.

Perhaps it was improper for her to speak.
But how pleased she was to encounter him
here—how beautiful she felt
in the dazzle of morning.

* * *

Later that day, they sat together on the wide
porch steps looking out onto the mountains.

It was the only day the men could rest.
Aaron had gone to town. Esther too
could do as she pleased, though her father
had commanded her to stay in her room.

But as soon as he had disappeared
behind the pines she ran to the steps
where Raymond was to meet her.

It was her eyes that undid him—black
and still and so sad they caught his breath.

After a while, in nearly a whisper, Esther asked,
What was it like? In France, I mean.

On the ride back to camp he'd told her
he was just home from the war. Esther longed
to know more but knew to wait.

Without hesitation, Raymond turned to her,
then looked down at his folded hands.

He paused so long that Esther
worried she had offended him.

An old Frenchie told me one night on patrol,
Raymond began shyly, *that they called it
the turnip winter, the one before we got there.*

His voice held like odd notes
in the afternoon air. Then he continued,

but something in his voice had changed,
as though he'd gone back there,
entered again that terrible time.

*Said it was the coldest he'd ever known.
Bread was ground up turnip and sawdust.
Godawful stuff, Frenchie said. When that was gone
they slaughtered the mule.*

Raymond took a deep breath and was done.

The two sat in silence as the windows behind them
flamed with the last of the sun's fire.

Esther held her gaze on Raymond's hands,
and Raymond held his on a clutch of crows
lengthening into dark fingers across the yard.

* * *

Aaron's delusions so blinded him, he did not
recognize how the air around his daughter

had brightened suddenly, or how she spoke—
when she did speak—in a lovely hush.

Nor did he recognize the grave young man
now so smitten he blushed when the other loggers

teased him. *Where's your girl?* they'd whisper,
elbowing him as he passed.

                    Aaron was lost to all of it.

She was his possession. He let that be clear.
And he didn't mind if the men reckoned
the extent of his hold over his daughter.

They would think him powerful to have
someone so young and so very beautiful.

But the men knew what he was—a bully
who took what he wanted because

it was his due. They thought it right
that someone got his chance with her
besides the old man.

Esther was the one good thing amid
the grueling work, the mosquitoes, a job boss
who could not be satisfied.

When they were quarrelsome, she put an extra
piece of pie in their lunch pails.
She made things right for the men.

* * *

Aaron was not a big man, but seemed
at times so dark a force that nothing

could escape the immensity of the affliction
that defined him, immovable, heavy as a house.

The men avoided him when they could,
minding his orders without question.

But if they got too close, calamity
seemed to hold them down, their posture

shifting to defeat, then desolation.
They would argue among themselves,
snarl at the least provocation.

These men had lived through much, but
had never encountered a man whose fury
                              turned to contagion.

Somehow Esther withstood the onslaught—
Aaron storming forward in one gulping rage
after another, she blunting his ugliness—

They had moved through her short life like this.
Even when she was no taller than the table,
and Aaron could scoop her up when desired
and spirit her away, she kept still.

Mother would be upset, the baby
might cry. Everything depended on her.

* * *

One evening a few of the men occupied Aaron,
gave him boasting room, so that Esther

and Raymond could meet. Aaron blustered
and gloated about his escapades in the border wars,

fighting Pancho Villa, he said, with his bare hands.
But the details made no sense to the men
who had really been there.

And that nigger lover Pershing, Aaron swaggered,
I taught him a thing or two.

One logger stood suddenly to protest.

Wait just a goddamned minute, he began,

but another next to him reached up with one arm
and brought him down hard, never

diverting his attention from Aaron, who
continued on, oblivious to the commotion.

Meanwhile, tucked in a corner of the darkened
kitchen, Esther guided Raymond's hands
to her face, his fumbling uncertainty
easing when she covered his hands
with hers, looked straight into his eyes.

* * *

Raymond's only encounter with a girl
had been terrifying—on leave in France.

He'd been led to where she sat
along a wall with other girls.

Small and dark-haired, she crossed
and uncrossed her legs as if
to keep herself awake.

He'd been so lonely for talk, but instead,
in the small filthy room she led him to, her mouth
turned weapon-like, as she *took care of him*,
as the madam had promised, then
spit on his newly shined boots.

Merci, Raymond said carefully, not knowing
what else to offer her. The girl's mouth
softened as she acknowledged his words.

But the madam entered in a storm,
took his arm firmly, and showed him
to the front door.

* * *

All week Aaron was encouraged to hold forth,
his tales becoming more and more

preposterous. The men nodded sleepily,
waiting for the one nearest the window to see

that the kitchen door had opened slightly, the signal
Raymond and the men had decided upon.

Just one more of Aaron's wild meanderings
and Raymond would be safely back in his bunk,
                              Esther in her bed.

* * *

In the dimness from one candle they dared
light, Esther and Raymond sat each night
at the world's rim, their need to speak
of what was deepest inside them
growing more palpable.

Raymond confided that what he had loved most
was his dog, and his horse, too.

And my books, he added sheepishly.

I've got one here in my pocket, he said,
and took out a tattered copy of *The Virginian*.

I've read it a thousand times, he said,
and with affection turned it over
in his hands, gently thumbed the pages.

Oh, yes, Esther said. *Yes. I have loved them, too,*
and told Raymond about the encyclopedia,

how it was secret, and that she'd read it
all the way through many times.
Their faces beamed in the candlelight.

* * *

By the end of the week, the two
had planned their escape. Denver was not far,
but how would they get to the train?

Once again the older men had an idea,
and by next morning, Esther and Raymond
stood on the platform holding hands, their heads

turned toward the train's approach.
Right on time, the locomotive thundered
down the track and into the station, enveloped

in billows of steam and screeching brakes,
until finally it stopped in front of them.

Fear ripped through Esther's stomach
but calmed when Raymond softened his grip
and brought her hand to his lips.

Her whole body felt suddenly that it was
where it was supposed to be.

* * *

The train was fancier than Esther was accustomed to,
with a large Pullman and an elegant dining car.

For a moment she wavered. Perhaps
they would get lost inside, separated

from each other. Or maybe they could
hide together and never have to get off.

But in less than an hour they were in Denver
station, passengers bustling, children bawling,
and everywhere the shrieking of whistles.

They walked from the heat of the platform
to the cool, gleaming interior.

Raymond went to look for a map of the city.
Esther studied her shoes. Aaron
had always thought her feet too big.

Why can't you have smaller feet? he'd ask.
She had no answer.

But she liked her feet just the same, and today,
in this place, she liked them especially.

* * *

Raymond returned smiling, a dark,
contoured bottle in each hand, the map
tucked under his arm. He guided

Esther to one of the long benches
crisscrossing the cavernous waiting room,
and handed her a bottle—*Coca-Cola*

embossed in cursive on its side. The thick
glass was so cold it surprised her.
Take a sip, Esther, Raymond grinned. *You'll like it.*

And she did, and liked, too, how
the seat curved under her body, as if
the wood knew to comfort her.

Raymond, Esther asked suddenly, *what if
Father finds us?* She turned away from him
and straightened her back. *You don't understand.*

Esther hadn't told Raymond about Aaron.
She hadn't meant to keep it from him exactly.
But when she was with Raymond
her father seemed so far away.

And how would she say it? How?

But Raymond already knew.

Charlie, one of the older loggers, had
taken the young man aside to warn him,
as it became clear that the two
were sweet on each other.

A small man, Charlie was the strongest
of the lot. He'd grown up in Louisiana,
and played harmonica with such tenderness

men sometimes wept—until
Aaron told him to shut the hell up
if he knew what was good for him.

*He'd just as soon kick you in the nuts
as say boo,* Charlie drawled. *He's the nastiest
son of a bitch I ever come across.*

And here's the thing, Charlie said,
taking a deep breath and choosing his words.

He treats his daughter like a wife.
Raymond looked at him, confused.

Charlie folded his hands nervously on his lap,
waiting for Raymond to catch on. *Son,*
Charlie said finally, leaning forward,

softening his voice, *he has his way with her.
And that's the god's honest truth.*

Raymond shot up onto his feet
looking ready for a fight.

Charlie motioned for him to sit down.
Raymond collapsed back into the chair.

I need to say one more thing, he said,
looking right at Raymond.

This Esther, he said firmly. *I don't care
what her daddy done to her, she's a fine girl.*

*Many's a man here who would still have her.
I'm too old, but if I was younger
I'd be proud to take her as my wife.*

* * *

In the station, Esther waited quietly
for Raymond to speak. Droplets began
to trickle down the icy bottle in his hands.

*I know, Esther. I know about it. Charlie told me.
But sometimes I don't understand.
Why didn't you say no? Why didn't you?*

* * *

Up at four that morning Esther had served
the men breakfast at six sharp: hash, biscuits
and gravy, fried potatoes, and stewed peaches.

While they ate in their usual silence
she packed their lunch pails,

placed a big slice of apple raisin pie
on top of each, wrapped neatly in wax paper.

Charlie knew he would not see Esther again.

You take care, hear? he whispered, as he
reached the door just behind Aaron.
When Aaron was out of sight, Raymond
slipped off unnoticed in the clamor.

Where's the kid? Aaron demanded,
when they reached the job site.

Didn't look so good at breakfast, Charlie
yelled over his shoulder, as he
helped unload the wagon.

Shit! Aaron spat. No one got sick on his crew.

At camp that evening, there was no supper
waiting on the long table, no heaping platters
or outsized bowls filled with hearty, fragrant
food steaming the windows.

Esther's room was empty, her clothes
gone. *She's with the doughboy*, someone said,
and stifled a laugh. This time Aaron heard.

* * *

Esther had left the makings for a simple supper
with instructions written on a small piece of paper.

The potatoes were already in a huge pot, peeled,
quartered, and covered with water.

Most of the men could not read—except Charlie,
who held the note in both hands as a small boy might.

Get the stove going good and hot, he read aloud slowly.
Matches are in the cupboard over the sink.
Charlie looked up to see.

The ham is in the ice chest, the fry pan
hanging right above you. Try out

a bit of fat first, then cook the ham hard
to brown. Father will like the darkest parts.

Aaron had been leaning against the wall
trying not to listen. He kicked himself straight,
swiped the paper out of Charlie's hands,
and stomped out of the room.

From the kitchen window, Charlie watched
him appear, then reappear in a clearing of bearberry
as he walked the perimeter of the camp,
once, twice, head down, arms straight at his sides.

Only his mouth betrayed him, opened
wide as he howled, but the wind took his
pain and heaved it down the mountain.

* * *

As Aaron walked, the sky darkened and a storm
gathered. Too late to go after them.
He'd have to wait till morning.

His quarters were next to the blacksmith shed.
A small wood stove provided heat.

Moving mechanically, he built a fire,
went deep into himself.

His ribald anger had turned to something
like grief, a weighing on his mind

he had never before felt. Esther
would not come back. He knew this.

He reached into his pocket for the rumpled
paper, studied the shapes on the page.

Then he placed it on the flames
where it flared brightly and died.

Once during the night, he thought he heard
her voice, but it was just the intolerable
wind whispering through the windows.

* * *

Aaron slept fitfully and dreamed of trains.
Great noisy beasts filled with people, conductors

bellowing last warnings and blowing their shiny
silver whistles, everyone waving goodbye.

He rose before sunup and dressed
in the dark. Denver. That's where they went.
He was sure of it.

By mid-morning he'd reached
the nearest town, found livery for his horse

and Esther's paint, told the leathered
stable hand he'd be a day at most, come back
with his daughter in tow. The man shrugged.

Aaron followed the tracks to the train station.
A glassed ticket booth sat in the middle
of the large waiting area.

He leaned in close to the speaking hole.
Which one's the train to Denver?

The ticket agent, in deep concentration,
was counting ones, licking his thumb
after each pile of ten. Annoyed, he replied,

Can't you read the sign? Aaron looked
around the station, pretending to read,
then turned angrily.

I just need a ticket, goddammit!

pounding the sill between them.

Well, why didn't you say so? the agent said,
never once looking up.

* * *

As the train pulled into Denver, he saw
Esther on the platform, a carpet bag

at her feet. Aaron leaned clumsily
over the stout man next to him and raised
the window. *Hey, hey! Over here!*

But when she turned, she was
some other girl, who, nevertheless,
waved tentatively.

He grabbed the luggage rack
and swung himself into the aisle.

What are you looking at? Aaron snapped
at the man whose lap he had invaded.
Mind your business, he grumbled,
or I'll mind it for you.

Then, as if the man had wanted to know,
had cared about the circumstances that
suddenly included him, Aaron continued,

*My daughter left with some doughboy.
A damn soldier! He's got no right, I tell you.*

She's mine, and I mean to get her back.

But the man had worked his way
halfway down the aisle by the time

Aaron noticed, and by then the train
was empty, too, as he stood there alone.

* * *

Esther and Raymond had walked away from
the sound of trains until they found a park.
Esther reached into her bag and brought out
two sandwiches, sliced biscuit, ham, and mustard.
Raymond's favorite.

The trees above them fluttered in a pleasant
breeze as they remembered the trip, as if it were
years before instead of that morning—

They laughed and took another bite of sandwich.
Then each fell silent. A heaviness grew
between them, but Esther felt it more.

She moved closer to him on the bench,
took his hand into her lap. She could feel
Raymond tense, and after a moment,

it seemed what sat next to her
was husk, as though he'd left his body.

What's wrong? Esther asked, the words
catching in her throat.

* * *

Along the platform passengers seemed
to Aaron to have somewhere important to go,
to withdraw from him as he passed.

A woman struggling with her bag
and two small boys rushed by him,

her body giving up its sweet, pungent
balm. Aaron remembered his mother

leaning in once to comfort him, her
smell as sweet and wholesome,
her bosom talcumed and soft.

But father put a stop to it.
Missus, he scolded, *let the boy be.*
You'll make a girl out of him yet.

Aaron sat on a bench, elbows on his knees,
and watched the woman hail a porter,
who scooped up her bag onto his dolly,
patted the two small heads, while she
searched her purse for change.

It began to rain. Gray sheets
swept across the platform. Suddenly
no one was in sight. The woman and her boys
had boarded the 12:40 for Cheyenne,
others taken cover from the downpour.

Aaron raised the collar of his jacket, held
onto his hat. The air turned clammy and dank,
and as if a door had clicked shut behind him,
he felt across his shoulders a tic of panic.

What would he do without his Esther?

Great swells pounded the landing
as he ran, silver curtains lifting, falling,
stinging his eyes, blinding him. The brim
of his hat flipped up from the force.

The train on the main track was ready
to depart. Several cars back the boys
quarreled over the window seat.

In the cab the engineer checked
the boiler pressure and water gauges,
the firer loaded the last bucket of coal
from the tender into the firebox.

One final check of his pocket watch,
and the engineer released the air brakes,
pulled the throttle slowly toward him.
He rang the bell and the train came to life.

He hadn't seen a man jump onto the track,
step up to the running board on the face
of the train, grab the handrail, then the grill
with both hands, and hold there
in the torrents of rain like an insect.

The engineer sounded the whistle at the first
crossing: two long, one short, one long, through
the second and third crossings, until
he was on the desolate outskirts of the city,
headed north under a full head of steam.

Flattened hard by the wind's force
Aaron struggled to straighten his arms
in front of him and with great effort
lowered his head back and let go.

For an instant the weight of his body
met the resistance of wind, and he hung there
balanced at an impossible angle. Then,
with another slight tilt backward

of his head, he fell, with a diver's
liquid movement, onto the track.

The train jolted hard a few times,
then smoothed out.

What the hell was that? asked the engineer,
peering out at a wall of rain.

Damned if I know, the firer answered.
We must have hit something.

Then both went back to their work.

Our Bed Is Green

—The Song of Songs

They'd found a boarding house
and Raymond nervously signed them in.

The room was small but clean.
He paced in front of the windows
while Esther unpacked their few things.

They'd barely talked about the future,
what they would do if they were
able to get away from Aaron.

And now here they were.

* * *

Raymond needed to walk, to shake
loose how Esther's eyes darkened
when she got sad or worried, how

something was tearing him up inside
but he did not understand what. Sounds
came to him, stuck in his mind—

his buddy hollering *Gas!* at Chateau-Thierry,
the guttering of the blinded boys marched
hand to shoulder to the dressing wagon.

More than once he turned to see
if someone were behind him, then
sunk his hands deeper into his pants
pockets and continued down the street.

* * *

Esther sat in their tidy room
and tried to imagine why Raymond
would care for her.

She'd nothing to give him, no dowry,
no land, no head of cattle, or father
to welcome him as a son.

Nor was she beautiful—like the girl
on the cover of her magazine: soft, dark
curls, perfectly bowed lips and brows.

She undressed to her camisole
and knickers and turned to the full-length
mirror, unpinned her black hair and let it fall.

She stood for a while taking stock
of what she saw—her broad shoulders,
strong neck and arms, ankles
just the right width for her body.

And her feet, despite Aaron's
insistence, were sturdy. And pretty too.
What a curious thing to say about feet,
she thought, and they were exactly that.

But her hair—the part of her Aaron
craved most—what use was it after all?

From her needlework she took tiny
scissors and began to snip—at first
cutting to her shoulders, then more, until
she'd fashioned a bob, which pleased her.

A ring of darkness surrounded her on the floor.
She stepped outside of it closer the mirror.

*You will never again feel his hands on you
or smell his foulness*, she proclaimed aloud

to the young girl who faced her,
speechless, in the glass.

Look back at my eyes, Esther,
whispered the girl. *Your escape will be
on the river of your tears.*

* * *

When Raymond returned, Esther
was curled up reading the Bible
she'd found on the nightstand.

Our bed is green, she read
from the Song of Songs. Smiling,
she patted the quilt next to her,
inviting him in.

Raymond slowly lowered himself
onto the edge of the bed.

What did you do? he asked. *What did you do
to your beautiful hair?*

Esther was stung by his question.

Don't be cross with me, Raymond, the burn
of regret nevertheless reddening her cheeks.

As Raymond persisted, Esther grew restless,

then so angry she began to cry.

Rattled by her tears, Raymond
drummed his fingers on his knee,
took a deep breath and let it out slowly.

Esther's shoulders and neck glowed
in the low light. He remembered
the first time he saw her, in the kitchen
at the camp—her lovely back exposed,
her skin creamy and moist.

Without meaning to, he reached out
and touched her breast, soft and full
under her gown, then ran his hand
up her arm to her hair.

Esther took his hand and kissed it.

I'm sorry, he said. *I'm sorry I hurt you.*

Esther had wondered what this would
be like, for a man to touch her this way,
a man who was not her father.

Night after night she'd dreamed of it,
to be taken with such yearning.

When he entered her, she turned away.
Please, Esther, Raymond said. *Look at me.*

* * *

Later that night, Raymond fell
into the blackness that haunted him.

Caught in a nighthorse, he howled
and gagged until the sheets darkened
with his sweat—the war
having opened its appalling mouth.

Esther tried to wake him, certain he was ill,
but his pathetic wailings only deepened.
A snarl curled his lip as he lashed out
as if someone were holding him down.

She slid off the bed onto the floor, lay there
on her back, everything blooming darkly,
unknowable, save the embering coals.

Raymond stopped thrashing and lay
curled in a ball, whimpering. Esther
held herself and shut her eyes.

* * *

The next day was Saturday, and all along
Curtis Street lively marquees of the picture
palaces were ablaze with traveling electric words.

On one marquee, Tom Mix, astride his sleek,
spangled wonder horse, Tony, reared up
triumphantly into a glorious western sky .

Let's go in, Raymond said, in sudden good spirits,
then took off for the ticket booth.

They had spent the day walking the city,
following leads for a job. Raymond insisted
that he could take care of them both,
that Esther needn't work.

What would you have me do then? she'd asked,
poking him playfully. He'd seemed unamused.

Now he walked excitedly toward
the grand entrance, resembling
a stage with its curtains pulled back.

When Esther stopped to touch
the silvery bow at the crease, she caught
the twang of her father's voice

warning her about such places, full of
sinful things a girl ought not to know about.
She quickly stepped back, and there—
amid a constellation of blinking lights,

the purple carpet runner, the velvet
tasseled queue gate— she froze—the old,
cloying dread pressing down.

Esther! Raymond yelled over his shoulder,
waving two tickets in the air. Her name
pierced the bruising dark, but still
she could not move.

Come on! he yelled again, but now

he was only a voice disappearing
into the thickening crowd. Esther turned,
and turned again, until his familiar face appeared,
until there he was, within reach.

Raymond, she whispered, the sight of him
already calming her. *Raymond*, she said,
gripping his arm, *don't ever leave me like that.*
Don't ever just walk away.

But he could not hear her in the din
as they floated into a sea of hats—straw boaters,
flat caps, soft-brimmed cloches.

Breathless, Esther looked back
to the place where she had stood, now
a knot of excited, smiling faces.

* * *

The lobby hummed with excitement.
The smells of popcorn and roasted nuts
and sweet cherry cider were thick in the air.
A dazzle of patrons waiting for the next
show chattered excitedly.

Raymond wanted to get as close
to the proscenium as possible, to sit
in the exact middle of the row
where he'd spotted two empty seats.

They squeezed themselves past
grumbling patrons, some standing
to let them by, others refusing

to move, so while Raymond crawled
over them in whatever way he could, Esther,
in a long, slim skirt, became trapped.

One woman, softening to this beautiful,
dark-haired girl, brought her knees
to one side to let Esther pass.

Go ahead, dear, she said softly,

lightly touching Esther's hand when
she did not respond. Esther found the
woman's eyes. *Thank you,* she said, hearing
her own voice as if for the first time.

Others in the aisle did the same,
and soon Esther was lowering herself
into the seat next to Raymond, whose
eyes were already fixed on the stage.

She sat still, her heart hammering, until
finally she dared to look around.

An amphitheater of plush seats
and wide-eyed faces surrounded her.

As the lights dimmed, the tips
of a hundred lit cigarettes filled
the cavernous hall with red stars.

From above the curved balcony,
a shaft of light swirling with smoke
shot suddenly toward the stage.

Laughter subsided when the *mighty Wurlitzer,*
as the marquee had promised, boomed
from behind an ornate grill near the stage.

The organist began in grand vibrato,
thundering up and down the scale so loudly

that Esther covered her ears. Then, the deep
bellow of a kettledrum, the clacking
of castanets, a twittering bird—
Esther was agog with wonder.

When the lights dimmed, the organ
quieted and the curtains parted with an
audible *whoosh*. On the screen, a lone cowboy
galloped across a rocky desert terrain,

a cloud of dust growing behind him.
Majestic snow-capped mountains
loomed in the distance.

Esther reached for Raymond's hand
in excitement, but his was pressed to his thigh,
tensing and releasing with each movement
on the screen, as the cowboy, in his outsized

hat, on his black, powerful horse, rode
into a bustling frontier town, dismounted,
and wrapped his reins effortlessly
around the hitching post.

* * *

With red upholstery and brass knobs
on all four doors, the shiny black flivver
shone so brilliantly Esther could see
her reflection as she, slowly,
admiringly, walked its length.

She asked Raymond once more
how they came to be driving
such a handsome machine.

A Mr. Holmes had put an advertisement
in the newspaper: *Experienced driver to transport
genuine automobile to California.*

Raymond admitted to the man that
he'd never driven an automobile but had been
a motorcycle dispatch rider in France
and knew something about engines.

Mr. Holmes liked Raymond right off
and took him at his word.

We're going to California! Raymond announced
on their third day in Denver.
Esther thought it a splendid idea.

Great Divide

We do not see things as they are; we see things as we are.

—The Talmud

Had Bessie sensed the malevolence
Aaron was ravishing upon their daughter
it would have been with a kind of knowing
handed down—which berries to eat, which not.

Who's to say why this was beyond her ken?
Even bluestem raked by the unforgiving
wind was, in all its commonness, unfathomable—

Now, sunset drawn clean and hot
along the edge framed Bessie as she endured
her life, never quite perceiving the shape
it nevertheless had taken around her.

* * *

Six months had passed without word
from Aaron, and though Bessie did not miss
his hard company, Esther's absence
grew each day more punishing.

She seemed chained to anguish
at the marrow, despair so palpable
she could not free herself.

Stricken with the ague, Bessie spun
in fevered delirium for four days.

Lela and William nursed their mother,
changed her soaked sheets.

How could I have let her go? Bessie moaned
at the worst. Lela had no answer.
But William said, *You didn't
let her go, Mother. Father stole her.*

* * *

Bessie had known about Esther's love
of the encyclopedia, though she never let on,
oftentimes busying the rest of the household
so Esther could slip off and be alone

in the parlor. Now Bessie stowed away there
herself when she could find the odd moment,
and when the children were to bed.

The day the young man delivered the set
she'd hurried the books two at a time
out of Aaron's sight, and would not

open them for fear he would somehow
know she'd been so foolhardy.
Now there was no need to be fearful.

At first she sat quietly, letting the day
slide off of her. Then late one evening,
she opened Volume A.

How dense the book felt, the leather binding
smooth and cool. Hidden deep, between
amaranth and *amaryllis*, was a small note.

When Bessie lifted it, a faint muskiness
rose from the page—

Inside the note was pressed a pale yellow
blossom that drifted down onto her shoe.
Mother, the note said, *please forgive me.*

* * *

Esther and Raymond left Denver full of plans.
They had fussed all the previous day,
mapping their route, gathering food
for the many days ahead of them.
California was a very long way away.

Raymond boasted that they were to begin
by traveling Route 6 over Loveland Pass.

Good God, man, don't go that route,
said the storekeeper as he packed
dried goods, marking each
off their list with a blunt pencil.

But Esther calculated that if the flivver
made it over the divide at the pass, and if
they did not run out of gas before the next

fueling station, wherever that was,
and if there were no late summer storms
in those mountains or flooding in the valleys
or bandits who wanted the automobile

for themselves, or if the mud were not
axle-deep and rain did not come down
as the locusts had, hard and terrible, and if,

when they reached the great basin,
their water held out and the grinding
boredom did not kill them or make them

cross with one other—and if they were
lucky, the beautiful black lizzie with red
seats and brass knobs would finally

reach the pass between the White
and Inyo mountains, to the lee
of the Sierras that plummet to the Mojave,
then on south through the high desert

to the San Gabriel range, and from there
descend into the lush orange groves
and nut orchards of the San Fernando Valley

to Los Angeles, where they were to make
delivery, and where, if all of this fell into place—
they would find their way home.

* * *

Dead three days, and Aaron was in no one's
thoughts. Esther understood he was to return
to the farm when the job was completed
and when she left the camp, it was very nearly so.

Bessie marked the time without Aaron
as good fortune. In her heart
she knew he was not coming back.

She'd taken in a boarder, a tall, soft-spoken
man named Drake with an almost indiscernible
limp, thick eyeglasses, and a penchant for snuff.

In return for his keep he was to help
Bessie on the farm, though he did not seem
to her to be a working man. He was refined,
almost formal in his miraculously white
starched collar and polished shoes.

Bessie Kennedy has taken in a star boarder,
Mabel Kutchen announced as loud as she pleased
at the greengrocer one day, and soon
the whole county believed it was true.

Bessie Pennington Kennedy, no husband in sight,
was providing favors for a strange man.

Mr. Drake worked hard, disappearing into
his room the moment chores were completed.
On one occasion he acquiesced to a pot of tea.
After the first sip, he asked Bessie
if he might relax with a dip.

It was a habit Bessie found undesirable.
Nevertheless, she nodded yes.

With a practiced move, he slipped his hand
into his breast pocket and brought out
a small silver box, flipped open the lid,

pinched a bit, and placed it into the webbing
between his thumb and forefinger. Then
he brought it to his nose and inhaled sharply.

He sat back then and closed his eyes.
After a long pause, he spoke. *My parents,*
he said, articulating as if Bessie would not

understand the language, *were missionaries,*
and we lived when I was a child
in a dreadfully poor village in India.

Bessie held her breath. *I once saw a tiger*
gnaw a man in half, he continued, opening
his eyes wide to the ceiling, as if
it were happening right there.

* * *

What was left of Aaron was now a dark
stain on the tracks, bits of cloth scattered
for half a mile, a flattened belt buckle
resembling a large brass coin, now
wedged under a crosstie.

His hat had been knocked off his head
on first impact and landed outside
the rails, safe in a patch of mugwort.

Some months later, two young boys
will come scuffling along the tracks
and discover a common tweed scally.

The boys will fight over whose bounty it is,
each pulling the hat until one falls
backward when the other loses his grip.

The winner will put it on his small head
and smile broadly, and they'll scuffle off
again, kicking whatever might move
down the tracks, the two growing fainter
and fainter against the far mountains.

* * *

The coupe had two side doors with gleaming
brass handles and crank windows, an oval
window in the back. The windshield
slanted stylishly under a sun visor.

Raymond held the passenger door
so that Esther could climb in and get settled.
But her skirt caught on the seat hinge
and when she tried to get free, she spilled

the contents of her satchel on the street,
spools of thread rolling in all directions.
An apple teetered on the running board.
They laughed for the first time in weeks.

* * *

They found Route 6 and headed west.
Raymond sat straight at the wheel,
his thick auburn hair lifting in the wind.
How handsome he looked, thought Esther.

Along the horizon the Front Range
glowed in late summer golds and lavenders,
some mountains still snow-capped.

They drove along Clear Creek into the canyon,
past Idaho Springs and Silver Plume,
the Never Summer Mountains due north,
Mount Evans to the south, slowly ascending
to the divide. Esther had read about
these mountains in the encyclopedia, that

a two-thousand-foot rise in elevation
was equivalent to traveling five thousand
miles north—animals and vegetation
adapted, molded by the harsher weather.
The idea had mystified her.

* * *

Here was the oakbrush of the upper
foothills, covered with canopies
of lodgepole pine, aspen on the south-facing
slopes, mule deer, and blue grouse.

Beneath black spruce spread bilberries,
Labrador tea, and green alder. Above the chaparral,
garlands of Douglas fir wrapped the ridges,
their spires offset by lances of light.

Through open high meadows
of bluebells and columbine, elk foraged
in bunchgrass up to their haunches.

Then, Engleman spruce and sugar pine, compressed
by altitude. Understory of gentian and sedge.
On the ascent to Loveland Pass, krummholz

a thousand years old and, above, alpine timothy
and spiked woodrush, whose roots grew deep
into rocky soil yet were so fragile even
careful footsteps could destroy them.

* * *

Over the bluster of the engine, Esther heard
a pair of horned larks, their high, sharp warbling
softening the stark landscape above timberline.

Yes, that was what she remembered reading—
a songbird where one least expected it.

Then, a white-tailed ptarmigan
in its mottled summer plumage scuttled
among dwarf willow, looking as precise
as the engraving she'd studied.

As they reached the summit of the pass,
Raymond was more quiet than usual.

Clouds were marshaling across a clear
crystal sky, delicate webbings like great
nets cast out over the canyons.

                             Cold grew bone-deep.
Cataracts of rain fell suddenly, and just as
suddenly froze into a thundering salvo
on the roof of the lizzie.

Raymond stabbed the brake pedal
and pulled off the road, covered his head
with his arms, and began to rock forward
and back, puling like a terrified animal.

Esther was thrown hard onto the dash,
her face hitting before her hands
could blunt the impact. Stunned
and confused, she sat shivering.

* * *

Everything became cloud-sifted, turning
the sky into a film of absorbed light—yet
under the vast plume of gathering storm,

adjacent peaks and lacy canyons between
remained clear and dazzling. A freakish
wind swept over the little car

and a discharge of thunder so
unrestrained it was naked sound, rain
slanting in great waves, hard rain

like the first rain, like the last rain,
punishing even what held on.

* * *

The two huddled there until the storm
gathered its robes and headed off.
Raymond slowly lowered his arms,
stared straight ahead, unblinking.

Esther spoke to him quietly.
You're here with me, she whispered,
not sure what else to say, or why she felt
so odd. He turned to her then, a peculiar
restlessness working his jaw,
and when he saw her bloodied face,

the gash above her brow, he opened
his mouth in horror, but only a rasping
came from his lungs.

Esther sat motionless, her hand
on Raymond's shoulder. Tears and blood
rivered down her cheek, though
she did not yet feel the pain.

Some time passed before Raymond
took out his handkerchief and gently
unfolded it. Then, as if he'd forgotten what
he meant to do with it, he folded it again,
stuffed the cloth back into his breast pocket.

He started the car and began the drive
down the windward side of the mountain
as if nothing at all had happened.

Esther's hand fell limp to her lap.

* * *

*Along the spine of the Rockies, the Great Divide
cleaved the continent into watersheds.*

*All sources of water—
precipitation and snowmelt forming lakes and streams,
rivers tumbling aboveground, slow moving
underground—flowed west to the Pacific.*

*Leaving the open slopes of the cordillera, fell-fields,
patches of heath and bogbirch, the landscape
was recast—the air warmed and softened, as moisture
on the westerlies brought lush swaths of forests,
dense, saturated, blue-green meadows
blanketing the downward sloping contours.*

*Small towns of Eagle and Gypsum, then the Grand River
descended into a breathtaking canyon,
where once an antecedent stream had cut through
sedimentary cover to hard crystalline core.*

These were the tablelands—mesas and plateaus,
starkly beautiful evidence of faulting,
folding— the continual movement
of the earth's crust. From the Cretaceous sea,
a swarm of discrete, thrust-faulted uplifts,

elongated, asymmetric welts, rose,
and through unrelenting erosion, rise still—
something in the mantle pushing them up.

Time—
its infinitesimal contortions, is all—no beginning,
no end, no way in or out. The stroke of its
outsized wing, the pounding of its huge heart,
carry them forward in their separate sleeps.

* * *

The canyon walls rose in stark majesty
a thousand feet above the roadway, a gravel path
on the north side of the ancient river.

On the opposite bank, a train traveled
east at full throttle. The engineer
sounded his whistle and waved exuberantly.
Raymond saw only the road. Esther
covered her ears and closed her eyes hard.

The canyon opened to a narrow valley, where
a bustling town spread out at the mouth
of the Roaring Fork, swift and deep.

In a grove of cottonwood along its banks
sat a small bungalow. A wooden sign
with a caduceus painted roughly on it
swayed in the yard overgrown with scrub.

Esther felt the lizzie slow and stop, but
held her head down and opened her eyes
just enough to see her feet, letting in only
the part of the world she could trust.

Raymond knocked tentatively.
When Doctor Benton came to the door,
Raymond regarded him suspiciously.

The doctor was drying his hands on a towel,
his sleeves rolled above his elbows. He was heavyset,
with a two-day stubble and wild hair.

A small child wailed from inside.
Esther widened her gaze to a man's worn
brown oxfords, one lace coming untied.

Well, young lady, Doctor Benton said, his voice
calm and resonant. *Looks like you need some stitches.*

His hand as he touched her arm
was warm through her sleeve.
Esther liked him right away.

He led her to a chair, a high-backed
oak that creaked when she sat. She kept still,
her eyes barely opened, sat small and dark,
as if she were shy. But she was not shy.
She had never known that feeling.

Doctor Benton pulled up a stool
to inspect her forehead
where blood had begun to dry.

What's happened here? Doctor Benton
asked Raymond, who was studying
an engraving on the waiting-room wall.

When Raymond did not answer, the doctor
cleared his throat. *Young man, what happened here?*
a tick of irritation in his tone.

Raymond turned as if someone
had called his name in a crowd of strangers.

It was a storm, Esther offered softly.
We hit a bad storm at the pass.
I'm not sure what happened after that.

Raymond returned his gaze
to the engraving—Saint Raphael,
his hands on a lame man's head.

The doctor told Raymond to remain
in the waiting area, then helped Esther
to her feet. *Come with me,* he said
as softly as she had spoken.

Esther sensed his composure as he guided
her into his office and onto the examining table.
His body moved with the unselfconscious
grace of her paint, ardent and sure.

Doctor Benton prepared a wet compress
and gently brought Esther's hand to
her forehead to hold it in place.
While he took her pulse, he appraised
her face and shoulders.

She wondered what his face looked like
and raised hers to meet his eyes—they were
large and velvet-brown, full of a sadness
that made them tender.

I'm going to have a baby, Esther said,
taking in her own words as she heard them.

Yes, I know, Doctor Benton said.

Weeper

What knows to do so dives deep as it can.

—Deborah Digges

The trail led her above and behind
the lake, so that when she first sighted it,
it hung below her, a bowl of clear
aquamarine hanging from the canyon wall.
Luminous, crystalline. Could it be real?

She'd heard about the lake, but never
imagined it would be in this unlikely
place so dazzlingly manifest.

They'd hiked all morning, stopping
frequently along the climb.
Raymond grew weary of the effort
and wanted to return to town.

For once Esther was defiant. She'd come
this far, and was not turning back now.
Angry, Raymond left her there.

I can do this, I can do this, she chanted
as she picked her way carefully down
through the dense underbrush and fern,
frightened yet determined.

She might have thought the scene
a mirage, the lake glistening, the sweet
hush of water falling in slender strands.

The air grew humid and pungent as
she reached the ledge, walled in by limestone
cliffs, leafy cottonwoods, lush overhangs.
Under her feet spread pale lacy rock.

* * *

The lake's rim was in continual
formation, groundwater faulting through
limestone beds, dissolving over millennia,

covering whatever it touched, to become
layer upon layer of calcite, so fragile
the oil from human skin could damage it.

* * *

Esther sat at water's edge, took off
her shoes and leaned out over her knees.
The sun and a few wisps of cloud
danced inside the lake and rippled
outward as she submerged her feet.

Reflected there as the water calmed,
she glimpsed a ghost landscape, beyond
the tops of her bare knees, her shoulders and face,
the bandage bright white on her forehead,
the cottonwood tree directly behind her—there,

piñon pines and the pearly encrustations
along the marshy shore fanned out in exact
duplication, upside down, but reflecting
back to her, leaning toward her gaze.

Mystified, she moved to another spot.
This new land followed her— pale shapes
draped in soft shades of gray—

a land no one else could see or enter.
She would carry it with her.

* * *

Next morning they were back
on the road. Red clay hills and sandstone
cliffs cut across the skyline.

The silence between them grew.
Penny for your thoughts, she said
brightly, summoning all she could
to be lighthearted. But her mind was
on the child inside her. Doctor Benton

guessed she was four months along. Already
her skirts were snug around her waist,
her breasts swollen and tender.

They're not worth a penny, Raymond replied sullenly.
Esther fell quiet again.

They reached the junction of the Grand
and Gunnison rivers. To the northeast, the stark
stage of the weathered book cliffs rose.

To the southeast, the Grand Mesa, to the west
a wall of canyons and monoliths. Between
these barriers, the Grand Valley spread out
with fruit orchards and ranches.

Raymond's spirits lifted as cattle came into view.
As he emerged the happiest he'd been in days,
Esther was folding and folding into herself.

She longed for the encyclopedia, her hiding
place behind the upholstered chair, all
the mysteries inside those books.

* * *

They found a fueling station next to the State Home
and Training School for Mental Defectives, its
windows barred, frontage scrappy with brush.

Raymond filled the tank and the extra
containers for the long haul ahead.
The storekeeper in Denver had warned them
about the desert. Folks sometimes
went off and never came back.

Raymond drove to the center of town,
stopped the car, came around to Esther's door.
He seemed even more grim and distant.

If we're ever going to make it to California,
he said, folding his arms, *you'll need
to learn to drive, to spell me while I sleep.*

She looked ahead at the confusion
of cars scurrying in and out of view.

* * *

*Star dunes, hummocks, flatirons
composed of Navajo sandstone, mudstone,*

*siltstone, windblown, ripple-marked
barchan dunes. Landscape transforming.*

*They were leaving the tablelands
and entering the Wasach Range at
the east edge of the Great Basin.*

*No water here will find the sea.
But how beautiful its containment.*

* * *

Esther was not prepared for the loneliness.
But she kept her secret. Only in rare
moments of calm did she allow the truth
to speak. The child was Aaron's.

She tried to imagine it as she remembered
baby Lela—sweet, fragrant scalp, tiny fingers
with impossibly paper-thin nails.

But all she could conjure was a coarse,
brutal man, his jaw set in a perverse
clamp around his pipe, a man
growing meaner inside her
every day, coming back for her.

What had been an adventure turned
to grueling, monotonous work.
Yet after a while, the desperate
familiarity proved oddly comforting.

Esther could sink back into the routine
of never-ending sky, the hot
breath of the desert engulfing her.

All there was to do was squint
and take in what would not be ignored.

When they were so tired neither of them
could drive, they would pull off, crank
the seats back, and try to rest. A few nights
they were forced to find a real bed. Esther
fell asleep instantly, clothes and shoes still on.

* * *

The heat on the road was intolerable.
It took every bit of moisture into its maw.
Esther's lips cracked and bled. She took off
her stockings, not the least embarrassed to be
that naked in broad daylight.

When she tried to talk, her brain went thick.
Raymond—she'd begin, her voice
trailing into the stifling air.

* * *

*Something had been lost. The land was slowly
starving. Bring with you what you need,
it seemed to say. You will not find it here.*

*Yet around them, shades of cream and gray, chamois
and gold swirled—this was the province*

*of basin and range—crustal shearing, abrupt
shifts in elevation, narrow faulted mountain chains
rising against flat arid valleys.*

*The two were caught in a pattern, but could not
see it, so helpless were they against its design.
They'd been driving through it for days.*

* * *

A scattering of greenish scrub came into sight.
Esther begged Raymond to stop. Beside
a rock pool a speckled salamander
blinked its bulging lidded eyes.

She cupped water into her parched mouth,
pressed her cool palm to her forehead.

Then in her belly the child moved.

* * *

Rising at last above brush sage as far as the eye
could tolerate, beyond saltbush, shadscale,
Mormon tea—mountains—and, if
their map were correct, California.

The pass seemed to lift the desert into another
realm, rising between the north-south chains.
Perhaps the mountains had formed
in this way, Esther thought, to provide
for them safe passage, and smiled
at the delicious impossibility.

So grateful were they for the cooler air, they
camped under a mountain mahogany, watched
the sun's glow deepen as it gracefully lowered
itself, until everything around them became
saturated with waning golden light.

In the astonishing quiet, Esther heard
the wingbeats of a small bird—a thrush
or a vireo—gone off to find a place to rest
until dawn—under the gnarled arm, perhaps,
of a four-thousand-year-old tree.

They rose earlier than usual, cleared the pass
as day broke. There, below them, spread
an immense, broad valley. Beyond, emerging
through a blue haze—the Sierras.

* * *

They had reached the Great Basin's far
western edge, a down-dropped block of land
between two vertical faults.

In the long past an eruption here had buried
much of the West—so colossal was its force
the magma chamber emptied to collapse.
A lobe of lava moved south and formed this valley.

The caldera—twenty miles long, eleven wide,
the west wall two miles deep—still grumbles
and shifts, deep beneath swaths of greasewood
and checkerbloom, Tule elk grazing.

A tribe called the Sheep People once roamed
this land, then Paiute—coyote's children.

Now the Paiute sit defeated on their reservations,
the piñon pine all but gone, their baskets—
rendered so efficiently from the land—
gathering dust in white men's museums.

* * *

They stopped at a diner and treated themselves
to breakfast of fried eggs and corned beef hash.
Too hot to eat, Esther sat quietly as Raymond
finished his plate, then reached for hers.

Out the window to the east the mountains
diminished, the land widened, and seemed
to go farther into itself. What called her
to this desert's rawness, Esther could not say.

She tried her best to convince Raymond. *Please*,
she said at last, laying her hand lightly on his.

I don't know why, but I need to go there. I must.

But he would not have it.

We just came from godforsaken desert, he argued,
stacking their plates in the center of the table,
folding his napkin.

Why in blazes would we do that again? Raymond said,

shaking his head as he reached into
his pants pocket for his wallet.

He paid the bill and they walked out in silence,
pausing briefly on the front step.

Then stay here, Esther said finally,
her voice darkening with imperative.
I'll be back in a day or two.

Wiping sweat from his forehead,
Raymond met her eyes.

To the west stood weathered granite
outcroppings, silhouetted against
jagged, opal shadows of the Sierras.

He stood motionless for a while,
following the trail of dust as the lizzie
headed into the Mojave, wiped his forehead
again, then walked into town.

* * *

The mountain the Paiute called Weeper
watched over Esther as she made her way
into a landscape of such harmony, it consumed itself
at the rate of its own growth.

She passed an abandoned mine, settling
back into the very land that provided
for the greedy men who had scrabbled there.

The tinkling of sheep bells, the bawling
of white-faced cattle grazing in the alfalfa,
gave way to an abiding silence.
Esther breathed it deeply into her body.

It was the dry season. Mid-afternoon.
A hawk skirred above the scrub.
Along the banks of a wash spread
a bosque of mesquite. Esther found shelter
under the canopy, the trees' dark arms
tangled against cloudless blue.

* * *

The elegance of interdependence —
living things exploiting and sustaining.
Swift adaptation exquisitely balanced
by boundless geological time.
In a swell of spring rain, fat bronze
water beetles and algae blooms
appeared in intermittent ephemeral pools,
while on a nearby slope,
a colony of creosote had thrived
twelve thousand years.

* * *

Pain had been coming on slowly
since the lake, tightening, then
falling faintly from her belly. Now
it rose and peaked, drifted off,
cycled again, harder each time.

Esther stepped carefully out of her knickers,
folded them neatly, lifted her skirt
over her head, then her blouse.
Her skin shone in the dappled light.

She cleared a circle of leaf litter,
mounded it in the center and sat cross-
legged there. The earth felt alive—in her
moist folds, along her warm inner thighs—
pulling, from her deepest sanctuary,
the life she had harbored.

* * *

Merciful dark descended into marbled
moonlight. A coyote approached,
tentatively, sniffed the ground, came
nearer, sniffed again, then sat.

Esther was not afraid.

Through the night coyote kept vigil,
shadow arms of the mesquite moving
slowly over its gray-brown fur.

Its baleful yellow eyes held fast
to the young girl, whose sorrowful moaning
hung thick in the air, who smelled of the earth
welcoming back what it had given.

* * *

In the rain shadow of the mountains, the desert
was infinitely inventive—some god inside,
coxswain of a longboat, guiding it
deeper and deeper into necessity.
It could not be, without such loss.

* * *

The lizzie had been out of sight
for a while now. Raymond found
the main street of town desolate except
for an old squaw sitting on the dusty

steps of a boarded-up saloon. Beside her,
a mongrel furiously scratched his hind end,
contorted in the throes of pain and pleasure.

The dog looked up at the strange man,
but the Paiute made no sign of recognition.
Her milky, blind eyes turned away
from her weaving, swift hands nevertheless
working the basket's design.

Raymond could not perceive
the courage of her life. Nor could she
his—the diabolical sounds of war
that rang pitilessly in his head.

He saw simply a filthy Indian, as
repulsive as the grit in his mouth.

When she did not acknowledge him,
he spat in disgust and moved on.

* * *

During the weeks of gathering, she'd hunted
quail and meadowlark for their bright
feathers, woodpecker for its red crest, dug

roots of the big pine. She'd harvested
devil's horn and sumac, willow and redbud —
offered thanks for their sacrifice.

Then the soaking and splitting, fragrance
of vanilla filling her, as the reddish
bark of the big pine was warmed.

From the elemental center, she designed
each vessel for its function — watertight
baskets to cook acorn soup, burden baskets
to collect the sweet nuts of the piñon.

As if she were a body in orbit, traveling
a galaxy of lupine and Russian thistle,
round and round her hands flew —
double, triple twining, coiling, weaving

warp to weft, calibrating the growing
circumference, finding the balance
her body knew between beauty and utility.

Sierras

Throw away the lights, the definitions,
And say of what you see in the dark.

—Wallace Stevens, *"The Man with the Blue Guitar"*

The next day Esther was able to clean
herself with what water she could spare.

She buried her bloodied undergarments
and as she did a sadness came down on her,
so heavy she was sure it would never lift.

The landscape that had sailed by
was now blurred to gray by her tears.
When she drove into town, it looked
even more desolate.

Her despair deepened at the sight
of Raymond, sitting on the diner steps,
unshaven, his shirt wrinkled and soiled.

It had been only two days, but he was
older somehow, as if he had given up
on the young man he was, traded him in
for this one—who was talking to someone,
but no one was in sight.

When she reached out her hand, he startled
as if he did not recognize her.

I have a stomachache, she said quietly,

wanting desperately to feel his arms
warm around her.
                        A puzzled look
brightened his face, but he simply
shrugged and walked toward the car.

The sun climbing into the dead heat
of the day framed Raymond's broad
shoulders with a blazing aura.

He could have been a god returning
in triumph to his kingdom.

For a fleeting moment Esther thought
to escape, but followed him slowly through
the dust he kicked up behind him,

past the old Paiute, whose hands
quieted as Esther neared.

* * *

There was a time of her first bleeding,
when she ran a mile east at sunrise, west
at sunset, to mark each of the four days
of her ritual isolation—a time for the shaman's
rattle, flutes made of elderberry stems.

There was a time of famine when she
survived on grasshopper and bitter herbs.

* * *

South through the arid valley
they traveled, along the lee side
of the Sierras. Peculiar clouds gathered
parallel to the mountains.
                                        Flat-bottomed,
rounded on top, they seemed stationary, yet
the wind howled below, leveling
saltgrass in its wake.

How could it be? Esther wondered. How
could clouds not be driven by wind as they
were on the prairie, their shape-shifting
dance across the sky, the corresponding
lift of the curtains—that one certainty?

* * *

The bumping of the lizzie hurt so, that
Esther curled into a ball in the back seat
and tried to think of something
other than the pain.

Eventually she drifted off into fitful
dreaming—her mother sitting in the parlor's
upholstered chair, behind which Esther sat
as she had so often, hidden and held

                    shield
safe by the aegis of its wings, gaslight
casting their secret across the floor.

Open on Bessie's lap was Volume A
of the encyclopedia. But instead of plants
or birds or faroff places, she read
as if to speak to Esther.

I hardly dare to think of it, Bessie read,
but an augury has come my way.

omen

And turning to her daughter, Bessie whispered,
Your father is dead.

* * *

When Esther awoke she remembered
little of the dream, just the sweet sound
of her mother's voice, the hard
lines of her face softened.

But something had washed over her,
had cleansed her mind.

Buzzards hung motionless in the bright
and vivid air. Here and there
sand had drifted into hummocks.

The extreme clarity of the desert,
the sun-blasted light, evoked in her still
a longing, but there was comfort in it.

A grove of Joshua trees spread
over a dry slope, each tree equidistant
from the other, laying claim to
just enough moisture to survive.

A member of the lily family, Esther
remembered, momentarily back
in her secret place in the parlor,
tucked behind the big chair.

That morning the smell of frying bacon
had filled the house, and even now,
she felt the slow rise of hunger,
which she welcomed.

She stayed still in the rear of the car
observing Raymond, his body supple,
his strong neck perfectly aligned yet fluid.

He seemed almost content.

* * *

On their journey's final mountain pass—
the San Gabriels to the south, Santa
Susanas to the north—high desert wind
was at their backs. It funneled downward
through the ranges and joined marine winds
from the Pacific, where the westerlies were born.

The windows of Esther's mind were
thrown open, all her many doors
came unlatched, as she and Raymond
descended—this time into paradise.

The valley lay before them, all else
preamble—wide and intensely green,
groves of orange and lemon and apricot,
fields of asparagus and melon
ripening under that sun.

They stopped to stretch their legs
at a vegetable stand just off the road.
A lush orchard spread for acres behind it.

Not far from the stand two men clung
precariously to makeshift ladders
flung up into strange gnarled trees.
They were harvesting some sort of fruit.

What are they picking? Esther asked the man
tending the stand, who sat on a rough stool,
a metal cashbox on his lap.

He was a small fellow with skin like glazed
mahogany and eyes black as her own.

No hablo el inglés, señorita, he said shyly,
then rose and waved energetically
to the men, cashbox clanging with coins
under his other arm.

No, no, Esther said, not wanting
to be a bother. *Please don't.*

There was some gesturing between the men,
then one climbed down his ladder
and loped toward the stand, smiling.
Esther repeated her question, wishing
she'd never asked it in the first place.

Why, those're olives, ma'am, he replied,
dusting off his hands on his overalls.
Then he reached for a large glass jar
on a shelf above baskets of potatoes.

Esther watched him closely, as he
screwed off the lid, took one for himself,
moved it around in his mouth, then
spat the dark pit on the ground.

Try one, he urged, holding the jar
in the air between them, his lips
and fingers shiny with oil.

Esther looked for Raymond, who had
been inspecting a bushel of peaches
and had moved on to the pomegranates.

Thank you, she said, turning back to the man,
and dipped two fingers carefully into the jar.
What embarrassment she felt faded

as she brought the olive to her pursed
lips, nibbled, then took in the whole of it.

Now it was the man who regarded Esther,
as she closed her eyes in pleasure.

Tears, she thought. *Tears* —

the sun and earth—and deep time,
the deckled edge of some far summer
waiting to burst, and does—

in so small a thing—all black
sheen and salt brine.

* * *

Beyond the orchard, beyond row upon row
of onions, alfalfa spreads to dry chaparral
on the fan slopes of the north range.

Something moves across this wide open,
bountiful land, so faint Esther cannot
quite catch hold of it.

They've come upon this valley as they would
a shepherd's bed of rushes, his outline
all that is left. This is the place of grieving,

its old song carried from mountain
to mountain, as the pendulum of day
swings slowly, irrevocably west —

until the sea hurls its colossal voice, warning
all who chance to come this far.

Once this river meandered unpredictably
through dense forests of willow and sycamore.
Along its banks grizzly bears roamed
among elderberry and wild grape.

What is now desert scrub was once
a jungle of thickets and dense woods. Vast
marshlands spawned heron and hooded
merganser, fox and bobcat.

Those lured by the promise of prosperity
planted vineyards and orange groves.
Cattle farms fed their increasing dependence.
And black gold gushed everywhere, bringing
greed and filth in equal measure.

Floodplain forests were cleared for
cultivation, trees cut for fuel, marshes
replaced by subdivisions and endless roads.

Now a city burgeons in this vast basin.
Now the river is a dry wash, its source
exploited before it reaches the surface.

The search for more water is all —

and when it is found, the land will
suffer the privilege of abundance.

* * *

For miles now, macadam, and more
and more bungalows on newly divided
land, a farm here and there looking
oddly pastoral among them.

On one farm two boys were flinging
squash against the side of a barn, cheering
as ripe vegetables splatted and sprayed.
Flesh and seeds stuck on impact, wallpapering
the barn with huge oozing flowers.

Raymond pulled off the road
and turned the key. He folded his hands
on his lap and watched silently. One boy
hung back, twirled around twice, hurled

the squash like a discus, screaming
with delight as it blew apart, all
stringy yellow and dark center.

They seemed to have been at it
for a while, shrieks growing louder
each time one exploded his arsenal, rinds
collecting on the ground in sad heaps.

What a waste, Esther said, expecting
Raymond to agree.

A long moment spread between them,
cold and cheerless.

Raymond responded finally,
almost under his breath.

They're not hurting anyone. At least for that.

* * *

The bungalow listed for rent was smaller
than they'd imagined, but it was clean
and furnished and near a trolley stop. And if
they found work, affordable.

The front entry opened into the living room.
Wide doorways in the center of the house
flooded the rooms with light and air.
No musty, dark parlor or drafty hallways.

The kitchen was small but efficient,
with a modern pump sink and electric stove.
On one wall stood a Hoosier cabinet. Esther

ran her hand over the cool white enamel.
Out the window above the sink,
eucalyptus and climbing roses, the house
fragrant with their scent.

She dug in her satchel and brought out
a weathered envelope, counted twenty dollars
in one-dollar bills, handed the owner
their first month's rent.

He was a land speculator who had
bought a ranch that once spread over
much of the southern end of the valley.

A boastful man, he never let the conversation
stray far from his many prosperous exploits.
He counted the money as he talked,
a feat that bemused Esther.

She was glad when finally
he reclaimed his hat and left.

By late morning they had moved in
their few belongings, then decided
to return the lizzie to its owner,
anxious to see the city.

They followed trolley tracks, their electric cables
dissecting sky. Soon the wires formed a chaotic
blue quilt, tangling at every intersection.

Automobiles honked and swerved, bells
clanged amid the drone of pedestrians
coming and going along the wide boulevards.

At every corner, it seemed, a bank
stood solidly, billboards in between
hollering for attention.

They parked in front of Samuels Dry Goods,
bolts of gay fabric in the window.

While Raymond struggled with directions
Mr. Holmes had given him, Esther
delighted in the jangle and glitter.

Across the street were assorted shops—
C. D. Crummins, Druggist, Fontella Cigars.

A large department store went up
four storeys. Stylishly dressed women
window-shopped, some drifting in.

Esther imagined the women chatting,
comparing hats, the elevator lifting
them gracefully—and wondered
what it might be like to ride.

* * *

They took the trolley back to the valley,
both of them exhausted, but relieved
to already have a home.

The sky was streaked red with flecks
of gold, as dark settled on their street.
Date palms rose from each front yard.
Silhouetted against the coastal mountains,
they disappeared slowly into blue-blackness.

As they approached their house,
a neighbor's mongrel came to meet them,
walking diagonally, as some dogs do, around
the lemon tree, and down their front path.

Small and wiry, he took an immediate liking
to Raymond, curling himself around his legs,
promptly falling asleep at his feet.

Esther had never seen Raymond smile
as he did at that dog.

* * *

For a time everything seemed to fall
into place. Raymond found work
as a roughneck on an oil rig, manning
equipment, piping down the well bore.

It was difficult, dangerous work,
but he was used to such matters.
Besides, it paid good money.

Esther did what she knew best,
and that was to bake.

New neighbors had also arrived recently
from the Midwest and Esther imagined
they yearned, as she did, for foods
they were accustomed to.

The first morning Raymond took the trolley
to his new job, Esther set to work on hers.
By noon she'd made an apple-raisin pie,
sweet-potato muffins, and biscuits, whose
light, flaky texture Bessie had taught her.

Be gentle and quick, her mother had said
patiently, *and not a stroke more than you need
to mix the dough, or you'll end up with
a pan full of paperweights.*

Now, at the Hoosier cabinet, flour
covering her apron, in her hair, Esther
laughed at the thought, just as she had
with Bessie, watching her sure hands
roll out the dough so swiftly
it hardly seemed possible—laughed

until her side hurt, until tears came,
and weeping, and a longing for her mother
flooded the little house, all
the bright rooms aching with it.

When Raymond returned home late,
wreaking of crude, Esther was sitting
in the dark kitchen, flour still in her hair.

More hungry than he'd ever been,
he let out a hoot when he turned on the light
and saw the pie and biscuits and muffins.
Esther laughed again in spite of herself.

The next day she rose even earlier
and got started before the sun.
By midday she'd filled a large picnic
basket with her bounty. One step
onto the front walk, however, and she
thought better of it. But soon
she was knocking on her neighbor's door.

*Hello, I'm Esther Arena Kennedy, and I
live in the house next door,* she said, timidly,
nodding in the direction of their bungalow.
Then she opened one flap of the basket.

Would you like to try one of these?

The neighbor, an older woman, with a sweet,
round face, peered into the basket and smiled.

My goodness, she said, looking up
into Esther's eyes. *What have we here?*

Vuelva a mí

Seek and learn to recognize who and what, in the midst of inferno, are
not inferno, then make them endure, give them space.

— Italo Calvino, *Invisible Cities*, translated by William Weaver

Two springs passed. Raymond was promoted
to driller, head of his crew on the rig.

Neighbors came to Esther's door now.
It was a rare day that any baked goods
were left, though when there were,
Raymond was grateful.

Their daughter was born, a bright,
happy baby, with Esther's dark eyes,
Raymond's sculpted lips.

At first Raymond was afraid to touch
Sarah, sure that he would
hurt her or drop her.

Esther showed him how to wrap her tightly—
that made a baby feel secure—how to
support her head with his hand.

Every encounter with Sarah seemed to
soften him, open him in a way
Esther had not been able to.

What do you suppose she's thinking? he'd ask,

when Sarah followed shadows on the ceiling
or found her fingers to suck.

* * *

When she was just two, Sarah woke
with a cough and mild fever.
She refused to eat.

The next day her neck began to swell.
Esther sent a neighbor for the doctor
who arrived too drunk to do much
but vomit in the gardenia as he left.

Raymond was on a three-day tour.
Esther had no way to reach him.

When he arrived home late
the following evening, the cloying
smell of disinfectant made him gag,

as it had when he was a boy, when
an epidemic took hold of his town.
His mother had called it the strangler,
and it could savage every last child in a family.

Raymond's case had been mild, but
it had taken Clara, his baby sister,

and so weakened brother Henry's heart
he had to be carried by their father.

Young Raymond tried to be patient, to sit
with Henry, read aloud as best
he could Henry's favorite stories.

But one day he left him alone to run
in the fields until dark as the song
of spring peepers filled the air.

That was the night Raymond
first saw his father weep.

All these years later he could
still feel that dreadful heaviness.

Henry had died during that long,
lovely afternoon and Raymond
was certain it was his fault.

Now, as he neared the bedroom
he could hear Esther softly singing.
He opened the door a crack,
afraid of what he might see.

Sarah's hair was matted from fever.
She seemed to Raymond smaller, more
fragile, but she shrieked robustly
then clapped her hands at the sight

of him—his face so blackened
with oil his eyes popped. Smiling,
she held out her arms.

Raymond gathered them both in his own,
generous tears filling his eyes.

Esther sobbed until she was done, then
a deep breath brought her back.

She stroked Sarah's head as she told
Raymond of the ordeal, how
she had found a doctor who had serum
and had taken it too just in case.

Then she lay down next to Sarah,
and the two drifted off together.

Raymond sat for a long while
watching them sleep, Esther's hand
fluttering imperceptibly in dream, the steady
rise and fall of Sarah's tiny chest—

and the house, too, was breathing, windows
wide, a storm gathering outside, shushing
the floor, stirring the edge of the coverlet.

Then, a nightjar's call.

* * *

Esther hired a Mexican woman
to help her with her baking.
Maria was small and cheerful, with
a broad face and infectious smile.
She knew little English, Esther little
Spanish, so they spent the first days

gesturing shyly. Within a few weeks
they could make themselves understood, haltingly,
melding two languages into one.

Ves? Esther would ask. *Do you see?*

Si! Yes! Maria said smiling. *Yo vea!*

Maria had seven small children,
and brought the youngest two with her each day—
the infant swaddled on her back, while
tiny Jose played contentedly with Sarah
alongside their mothers in the kitchen.

* * *

Across the land the golden sun comes down
to meet the new green earth, its loamy
heart all wild desire.

But even in this amplitude of light,
something dark rises—dextral, strike-slip,
beneath these transverse ranges.

Too late for prophecies—blind
thrust of that which is invisible.

* * *

With a roar like a hundred express trains
racing over their heads, the well blew out—
spewing crude in all directions. Raymond
was some distance away checking pipe
for the next day's bore.

Lights out! Lights out! he screamed, but
the hillside had already leapt into flame.
A nail in the roustabout's shoe scraping rock
was all it would have taken.

The derrick writhed and twisted, casings
wilted. Men were charred where they stood,
and Raymond watched, helpless

to make it right, their bodies
contorting—not of their will, but as if
some wretched puppeteer were
making them dance.

It took a hundred men a week
to get the fire under control.
Then they began cleanup.

Raymond stayed on site, bunked
with the other drillers. He sent word
to Esther, a note neatly penned.

I must stay here, he wrote, *until
my men are accounted for.*

Please take care of our beautiful Sarah.
                                    Raymond

Esther folded the note and put it
in her apron pocket, and at the end
of the day, she put it under her pillow.

And so it went for the time Raymond
was gone, the note unfolded,
read, and reread.

The men's families came to recover
remains. Raymond obliged them
in whatever way he could, helping
make arrangements, letting one father

tell him over and over how his son had been
such a good boy, such a good boy.

Raymond knew the smell, knew
how to push it as far back as it took
to do what needed to be done.

Not until the fire was safely out
and the grieving went home to reenter
their lives, did he agree finally to leave.

A few people waited at the trolley stop.
Across the street two men—workers
in overalls and caps—began to shove one other
angrily and shout. Beyond them, a crowd

moved like a many-legged beast, lurching,
halting. Raymond's own legs felt suddenly
thick, but he ran hard, and when

he found an alley between two buildings
he bent over, lungs searing, hands on his knees.

When he caught his breath, he
made his way to another stop, but there, too,
a group of men had gathered,

hollering and jeering at any passerby
foolish enough to get too close.

Strike! Strike! they shrieked. *Death
to the open shop!*

A young thin one emerged, his teeth
bared, and Raymond was back in the war,
bayoneting a soldier no more than twelve,
enemy trenches in those last days
filled with old men and boys.

For three days he did not speak,
and when he did, his words made no human sense.

Then one evening Raymond raised himself
wearily from the dinner table, disappeared
behind the viburnum at the edge

of the path—and never came back.

* * *

For a month, Esther fed and bathed Sarah,
read her to sleep, then made dinner for herself
and Raymond, set the table for two.

Night after night she sat alone,
as dark overtook the valley.

Finally, she took Raymond's plate away.

* * *

She had sometimes felt as if Raymond
were an apparition, floating
in and out of the rooms of her life—

and now, in crushing loneliness, his face
interposed in her mind—as clearly
as if he were there with her.

But when she was not thrown down
so far by his absence that she drowned
in the dolor that flooded her, not stilled
by the sudden, frightening anger—

she would let herself remember how
he'd come to her that day in the meadow,
wraithlike at first, then in full measure
against the wide sky, his man smells
mixed with leather and horse.

Here she stayed as long as
her mind would allow, until Maria
touched her arm. *Vuelva a mí,* she would say.
                              Return to me.

Slowly, painfully, the body she
dressed each morning, undressed
each night, became her own again.

* * *

But something had changed. The future—
if there were to be a future—had slid
like a water bird under the surface of its world,
to reemerge sleeker, inconsolable.

Queen of the Meadow

The past is never dead. It's not even past.

—William Faulkner, *Requiem for a Nun*

Esther stood motionless among swooning
believers, their arms raised toward the healer,
who, kneeling now, swayed, spread her arms
wide to welcome the Spirit.

The Savior is here! shouted Sister Aimee.
Praise the Lord, Jesus!

And the believers raised their arms higher.

Speak! Sister commanded. And they spoke—

in swells of sound, lark-like—
a language Esther had never heard.

Their eyes closed, some weeping, some
smiling—they seemed beguiled
by a force sweeping over them.

Even the Almighty played second fiddle
to Sister Aimee. Above her Angelus
Temple, a rotating, illuminated cross
was visible for fifty miles.

Inside, a choir of one hundred voices,
and Radio KFSG Los Angeles, proclaimed
Sister's Foursquare Gospel's message.

In the Miracle Room, wheelchairs,
piles of crutches—proof of Sister's cures.

Descending a gleaming white staircase
to the stage, she gathered her adoring flock
for the heavenly rewards awaiting the righteous.

Behind her, the spectacle
of the evening's illustrated sermon—
through booms and flashes of a piped-in storm,
a dozen night-gowned maidens, who clung
to a papier-mâché Rock of Ages, were
dragged to safety by sailors of the Lord.

Accept your loving Father, Sister intoned.

Let his Holy Spirit enter you!

Aimee Semple McPherson wanted
Esther's soul. But Esther would not submit.

    * * *

Esther floated into the bleakness
of her evenings—whatever she could not bear
in daylight coming at her in waves.

Once a young girl materialized—Lela—
twelve when Esther left the farm.

In the small bedroom they shared, Lela
had learned to lie quietly until their father
had finished with Esther. Then one night
he turned to the younger girl.

Esther meant to protest, to save her sister
from the stink of his tobacco hands, but
weariness took her to the wide river of dream.

Next morning she asked her parents
if she might sleep in the attic gable.
Aaron would follow her, she reasoned
to herself, and leave Lela be.

Ruth is almost weaned, she insisted,
when her father balked. *The bedroom
will be too small for three of us.*

As Aaron's mood darkened,
Bessie seemed relieved.

But Esther knew the plan would not last.
So when Aaron announced his scheme
to work at the lumber camp, to make

a year's worth of money in a summer,
and would not leave without his eldest
daughter, she agreed to go.

Now, yoked in loneliness, her castle
and moat, her welcoming stone hearth
mere lithic scatters, she remembered

Lela's eyes that night, pleading
with her to stop him. But in the airlessness,
something had pulled Esther under so far,

she hardly heard the creaking
of her younger sister's bed, their father's
loathsome moaning, hardly saw his
buttocks calving in the half light.

When she and Aaron left for Colorado—
his arm around her neck as if he meant to
bring her down as he would a calf—Lela

fled to the safety of the canning cellar,
where she and Esther had stolen away
on hot summer afternoons.

That was the last time she saw Lela,
disappearing into the dark, arms crossed
tightly over her chest, her cheeks
streaked with tears.

Then a sinister thought tightened
in Esther's gut. Father had gone back for Lela.
He had gone back to get her.

* * *

That night at the kitchen table Esther
counted the money she'd saved
in the crockery jar, wrote $127.52
on a scrap of paper, laid her pencil down,
and stared at the sum for a long time.

The clock ticked imperceptibly
as her mind tangled with thoughts.

Surely it was enough to buy one train ticket
to Independence. Sarah could sit on her lap.
But what if Aaron were there?

She rehearsed over and over what
she would say to him, the words sounding
more hollow with each imagining.

Then a wave of strength washed over her.
What more could her father do to her?

Oh, but Lela. *Lela.*

* * *

Esther had vowed she would never again
board a train like this one, never return
to Bessie or the farm, where the memory
of betrayal still flowered in terrifying clarity.

But now she was hurtling toward
the inevitable, tracks once again cleaving
the horizon. Nothing could stop her.

As they began to cross the prairie late
into their third day, a deep violet haze
fell on the land, tendrils of rose-tinted clouds
trailing under the brilliance, the rim of the earth's
shadow offering the last line of light.

Esther had forgotten how she loved
this simplicity, how, when she was a child,
her mother had set chairs facing west

to watch the sun set over the pasture,
the one cottonwood rising triumphantly
into the diminishing day.

* * *

Independence hadn't changed except
for automobiles clogging every street.

What was once the livery
was now a fueling station.
Next to the station was a cabstand.

Esther asked the driver slouched in the front seat
if he knew how to get to the Kennedy farm
south of town. He nodded.

The man had narrow-set eyes
and a thin neck and his hair combed
over his head from one ear to the other.

You've been gone a while, he said matter-of-factly.
Turning a hard stare on her, he took the cigarette
from his lips and flicked it into the street.

Why, yes. Yes, I have, Esther replied,
feeling her face flush.

From the back seat she could see his
one eye in the rearview mirror hold to the road,
then shift to her, then back to the road.

He headed out of the village and drove
for a time, then turned into a dense thicket
of sycamore, which, Esther remembered,
opened to the dirt lane that led to the farm.

Stop here, driver, Esther said firmly.
We'll walk the rest of the way.

She gathered Sarah and their belongings,
paid the man his fare, watched him
pull back onto the road.

Just before he rounded the bend
he stuck his head out the window,
that comb-over flapping in the wind.

* * *

Esther rearranged the bags
and with her free hand took Sarah's.

The child searched her mother's face
for clues. She was only five, but she
knew things, knew now to be silent.

Through the trees the old house
was broken into bright shapes.
Someone had painted it yellow, Bessie's

favorite color. She'd have had every room
yellow if she'd had her way. But Aaron
forbade such fancies. It'd look like
a goddamn sunflower, he'd growl.

Esther heard still the disgust
in his voice and shivered.

The barn emerged, scrappy and familiar,
and beyond it, the north pasture
already awash with morning,

a gauze of golden light hovering
over the nimblewill and wild rye,
the cows put to grazing there.

Bottomland along the creek was still
dark with walnut and hickory.

What Aaron had brought under
his thumb now seemed untroubled, the air
softer. Slowly, then, Esther understood.

Her father was not there, was not anywhere
near. He had never come back.

* * *

The dooryard came into view, the picket gate
unlatched. Deep pink flowers bloomed
tall against the house. Folks called them
Joe-Pye weed. Bessie had crowned them
Queen of the Meadow.

How those little victories had lit up
her sad long face.

Under the crape myrtle at the corner
of the dooryard was a headstone.

Esther had always imagined her mother
resting in that cool, stippled light,

her promise kept—that one day
she would lie under that tree.

For a moment Esther was back
with her mother— a time in apple season
when she was ten.

Father was to be gone a week, bringing
shoats to market. A sense of merciful calm
drifted onto the farm. Harvest was upon them,
the well four men deep.

The booming grounds of the prairie
chickens were askitter with chicks.

That morning Esther bundled the baby,
already plump and smiling, into the carriage,
and with Lela and older brother William,

set off to gather windfall apples for apple butter,
growing happier as the day unfolded.

By afternoon they'd put their hands to coring
and peeling, while Bessie cooked and sieved.

Taste, she would say, and gave them
each a big spoonful from the bubbling pot,
touching their cheeks as if to bless them.

Now the river coursing through Esther
brought grief and release.

* * *

Sarah counted butterflies visiting
the larkspur. Growing restless, she toed
the dirt in a circle with her buckle shoe,

tugged gently to be let free
into the kitchen garden, where
a young woman wearing a wide-brimmed
hat bent into a bed of purples and greens.

Still deep in thought, Esther followed
Sarah, stopping at the low hedge of box,
and stood for a long while
watching the woman.

She was humming in the reverie
of her work, somewhere vast
and boundless, where, it seemed for a moment
the world had dropped away.

Only the wind now and humming—simple
human mettle buoyant in the sunlight.

Neither happiness nor unhappiness
inhabited that garden, just the lovely
quotidian of day.

The young woman stood up
and took off her hat, fanned herself in the heat.
She sensed someone and turned and, after
the briefest interval, smiled.

It was then that Esther saw it was Lela,
grown strong and comely, thick
auburn hair framing her face.

Behind her Sarah wandered contentedly
in the lush rows, her arms outstretched
in marjoram and sage, their savory
sweet fragrance rising.

* * *

The earth stirred beneath them,
infinitesimally, circling and circling

back to a time before wind
raked the prairie, before sweet corn ripened
along the lowlands—

to when this garden— prevailing, its velvet
cry, taproot going forever deep—was an idea
that would not hold still.

Acknowledgments

My deepest gratitude for the guidance and support of all the friends, family, and fellow writers who have helped me navigate the long struggle to draft this manuscript. Thanks also to Burdicks in Walpole, New Hampshire, where I sat each early morning in the summer of 2012 as *Esther* took shape— and to Jill Marquess, Carolyn Ingraham, and Beth Kahmi for teaching me so many things.

CavanKerry's Mission

CavanKerry Press is committed to expanding the reach
of poetry to a general readership by publishing poets
whose works explore the emotional and psychological
landscapes of everyday life.

Other Books in the Emerging Voices Series

Love's Labors, Brent Newsom
Places I Was Dreaming, Loren Graham
Misery Islands, January Gill O'Neil
Spooky Action at a Distance, Howard Levy
door of thin skins, Shira Dentz
Where the Dead Are, Wanda S. Praisner
Darkening the Grass, Michael Miller
The One Fifteen to Penn Station, Kevin Carey
My Painted Warriors, Peggy Penn
Neighborhood Register, Marcus Jackson
Night Sessions, David S. Cho
Underlife, January Gill O'Neil
The Second Night of the Spirit, Bhisham Bherwani
The Red Canoe: Love in Its Making, Joan Cusack Handler
WE AREN'T WHO WE ARE and this world isn't either, Christine Korfhage
Imago, Joseph O. Legaspi
Through a Gate of Trees, Susan Jackson
Against Which, Ross Gay
The Silence of Men, Richard Jeffrey Newman
The Disheveled Bed, Andrea Carter Brown
The Fork Without Hunger, Laurie Lamon
The Singers I Prefer, Christian Barter
Momentum, Catherine Doty
Imperfect Lover, Georgianna Orsini
Soft Box, Celia Bland
Rattle, Eloise Bruce
Eye Level: Fifty Histories, Christopher Matthews
GlOrious, Joan Cusack Handler
The Palace of Ashes, Sherry Fairchok
Silk Elegy, Sandra Gash
So Close, Peggy Penn
Kazimierz Square, Karen Chase
A Day This Lit, Howard Levy

Printing this book on 30-percent PCW and FSC certified paper saved 2 trees, 1 million BTUs of energy, 127 pounds of CO_2, 67 pounds of solid waste, and 524 gallons of water.